EUROPEAN
CLOCKS AND WATCHES
IN THE NEAR EAST

STUDIES OF THE
WARBURG INSTITUTE

EDITED BY E. H. GOMBRICH
VOL. 34

O. KURZ

EUROPEAN
CLOCKS AND WATCHES
IN THE NEAR EAST

LONDON
THE WARBURG INSTITUTE
UNIVERSITY OF LONDON

1975

E. J. BRILL
LEIDEN

© THE WARBURG INSTITUTE, 1975

ISBN 0 85481 053 6
90 04 04326 8

PRINTED IN THE NETHERLANDS

BY E. J. BRILL — LEIDEN

CONTENTS

PREFACE

Had somebody in the Middle Ages announced a book with this title, the public would have misunderstood him completely. They would have assumed that "European clocks and watches in the Near East" was a proverb, or proverbial saying, of the "Owls to Athens" or "Coals to Newcastle" type, the description of the futile action of carrying something to its original home or to the place where it already exists in abundance. For many centuries Europeans regarded the Islamic East as the land where horological knowledge was at home, the source one had to approach if one wanted to study the science of exact time-measuring.

How and when did the East and West change their respective parts, and the pupil become the teacher? How did the West acquire its technological superiority in this particular field?

Many years ago when reading about the Moroccan embassy which arrived in London in 1600, I was surprised to learn that an attempt was made to sell them English scientific instruments, and that the point was made that these could easily be provided with the necessary Arabic inscriptions. I had seen and admired astrolabes and other instruments from North Africa and other parts of the Islamic world. To sell English ones to the Moroccan visitors seemed to me as odd as if one had tried to sell them camels.

I was also familiar with the Turkish watch dating from the seventeenth century in the former Imperial collection in Vienna, which is signed by two men with European names. It was not an isolated instance; gradually I came across more and more watches made "for the Turkish market", but I made real progress only when I stopped making notes of every single one, because by then I realized that hundreds of thousands of them existed.

In a lecture given at the Warburg Institute in February 1973 I tried to interest others in a subject which seemed to me worth pursuing. When afterwards the Director, Professor Sir Ernst

Gombrich, kindly offered to publish my study, I felt not only proud but also highly gratified because at the moment of retirement this would be my valediction to an Institute where I had spent my whole working life.

I gratefully recall the help given me by my friends and colleagues (these words are synonyms) at the Warburg Institute, as well as by my friends outside, and I want to thank particularly Professor Richard Ettinghausen for constant encouragement; Professor Paul Wittek for much, but not enough, biting criticism; Professor Gershom Scholem for translating and explaining to me a difficult passage from the *Zohar*; Dr. Arthur Bergmann for stimulating discussions and for permission to reproduce clocks and watches belonging to the Laura Julia Foundation, and now on loan to the L. A. Mayer Memorial, Jerusalem; and Dr. A. E. Hollaender for helping me with the manuscripts in the Guildhall Library.

Mr. Hugh Tait kindly allowed me to work in the Horological Students' Room of the British Museum, where I was constantly helped by Mr. Beresford Hutchinson. I am much indebted for information and photographs to three horological experts in Germany, Dr. P. A. Kirchvogel (Kassel), Dr. V. Himmelein (Stuttgart), and Dr. K. Maurice (Munich).

In the final stages of this volume I would have been helpless had not two friends come to my rescue: Anne Marie Meyer who gave up much of her time to achieve the metamorphosis of a manuscript into a printed book, and J. B. Trapp who went carefully through the text and translated a number of passages from the original King's English (George I's, to be precise) into the Queen's English.

The staff of E. J. Brill produced this book with a perfection and at a speed which would have been considered incredible in a former age, and seems a miracle in our own day.

LIST OF ILLUSTRATIONS

Sources of photographs are given in brackets. Grateful acknowledgement of permission to reproduce is made to the authorities concerned.

INTRODUCTORY CHAPTER

THE AGE OF ISLAMIC SUPREMACY

1. THE CLASSICAL HERITAGE: GREEK SUNDIALS AND WATER-CLOCKS

Time-measuring in mediaeval Islam is a chapter in the history of the classical tradition. The Greeks knew of two ways of telling the time: the sundial and the water-clock.

The sundial is based on two elementary facts: that the shadow is shortest at noon, and that it changes its direction according to the time of the day. But that is not all. The hour-scale changes according to the time of the year. And as the Greeks had not only sundials fixed to buildings, but also portable ones to be used when travelling, it was necessary to adjust the latter according to the geographical latitude[1]. Greek mathematicians enjoyed constructing more and more complicated sundials, but they were not the original inventors. We learn from Herodotus (II, 109) that the sundial was of Babylonian origin.

The water-clock, on the other hand, was apparently an Egyptian invention[2]. It possessed the great advantage that it indicated the time even at night, or in daytime when the sun was not visible. But unlike the sundial it needed constant attention and refilling[3]. In its simplest shape it is a water vessel with a hole in its wall. The water leaks out at a slow and regular pace, and a scale on the wall indicates the passage of time. Greek engineers invented many refinements to transform this simple device into a complicated automaton. The water could be made to move floating gadgets which in their turn would move human figures;

[1] By far best survey of classical sundials is H. Diels, *Antike Technik*, 2. Aufl., 1920, 160 ff.

[2] L. Borchardt, *Die altägyptische Zeitmessung*, 1920 (*Die Geschichte der Zeitmessung und der Uhren*, Bd. 1, Lief. B); A. Pogo, 'Egyptian Water Clocks', *Isis*, 25, 1936, 403-425.

[3] On classical water-clocks see again the excellent survey in Diels, *l.c.*, 192 ff.

it could move wheels, or the compressed air could be made to escape through a kind of organ-pipe and produce sounds. If one combined the mechanism and the sounds, as Ctesibius was the first to do, one could construct water-clocks with human figures which played a musical instrument, e.g. a flute or a horn. Equally attractive were mechanical singing birds, or—as children and grown-ups love some kind of *frisson*—hissing snakes. The whole thing was a wish-fulfilment, the old dream of life-like sculptures which had the power of moving, and were even provided with voices.

Our survey of Greek time-keepers would not be complete without mentioning bedbugs. According to the Stoic philosopher Chrysippus everything in nature has a definite purpose, and the purpose of bugs is to prevent us from oversleeping [1]. The place of bugs in the plan of creation is a fascinating subject and much could be said about it. If I do not pursue it here it is with great reluctance and simply because I feel that only Voltaire's Dr. Pangloss could do justice to its many philosophical and theological implications.

2. THE CLASSICAL HERITAGE: THE "SINKING BOWL" WATER-CLOCK

There exists some linguistic, but no other, evidence for the assumption that the "sinking bowl" water-clock was a classical invention. No one has ever found a reference to it in Greek or Roman literature, and no such bowl has turned up in excavations. Some scholars have claimed that perforated bronze vessels from Iron Age England and Ireland were water-clocks of this type, but this seems most improbable. Even the unavoidable Druids have been brought into this context [2].

The "sinking bowl" is a water-clock, although it functions on

---

[1] Plutarch, *De Stoic. repugn.*, xxi, p. 1044d (*Stoic. vett. frgg.* 1163).

[2] E. W. Hulme, 'Currency Bars and Water-Clocks: the Verdict of Archaeology Reviewed', *Antiquity*, 7, 1933, 69-72; reply by R. A. Smith and rejoinder by E. W. Hulme, *ibid.*, 210-215. F. A. B. Ward, *Science Museum. Descriptive Cat. of the Coll. Illustr. Time Measurement*, 1966, No. 9.

the opposite principle: instead of emptying its contents, it is gradually filled with water. A bowl with a small hole in the centre of its base is kept floating in a basin. The water percolates through the aperture, and gradually fills the bowl which after a fixed time-interval will sink down. Somebody has to watch it, and to announce the moment of its disappearance by striking a gong.

The sinking bowl is, or was until recently, much used in North Africa[1], Persia[2], India and Further India[3]. In North Africa, especially in Algeria, it was mainly used for measuring the time for irrigating the fields wherever the supply of water had to be strictly rationed. In India its use is old, but it is impossible to say how old[4]. From there its use spread both to Burma, where it was used in the Emperor's palace at Mandalay, and to Malaysia where instead of the usual metal bowl a pierced coconut shell was employed[5].

It remained unknown in some parts of the Islamic world. Babur, the first Mughal emperor and conqueror of India, described in his autobiography the Indian usage of it as something remarkable and new to him[6]. Its occasional use in Catalonia is evidently due to influence from Islamic Spain[7]. Perhaps one should add that the sinking bowl did not always remain a primitive

[1]   Ward, *l.c.*, No. 10. Photographs of Algerians using such a sinking bowl can be seen in Diels, *l.c.*, pl. 16, and in D. de Carle, *Horology*, 1965, pl. 2b. Th. F. Glick, 'Medieval Irrigation Clocks', *Technology and Culture*, 10, 1969, 425.

[2]   H. E. Wulff, *The Traditional Crafts of Persia*, 1966, 235.

[3]   One should add that it was at one time known in China, but there its use seems to have been very rare. J. Needham, *Science and Civilisation in China*, III, 1959, 315 n.

[4]   All the early literary references seem to refer to clepsydras of the normal type, as has been pointed out by J. F. Fleet, 'The Ancient Indian Water-clock', *Journal of the Royal Asiatic Society*, 1915, 213-230.

[5]   The Pitt-Rivers Museum in Oxford possesses characteristic examples from Mirzapur and from Mandalay, and a model showing Malay boatmen measuring the time with such a coconut shell.

[6]   He reformed at once the not very practical system of announcing the time by strokes of the gong. Babur, *Memoirs*, transl. by J. Leyden and W. Erskine, 1921, II, 239.

[7]   In an eleventh-century manuscript from Ripoll (Ms. 225) a certain method of surveying is described where time is to be measured with the help of an astrolabe or, as an alternative, a sinking bowl. The bowl had no time-scale, and the context makes it clear that the device was not in everyday use. The text itself has been edited by J. M. Millás Vallicrosa, *Estudios sobre historia de la ciencia española*, 1949, 71.

instrument for measuring time. Islamic technicians managed to incorporate it, or rather its principle, into their complicated automata [1].

In Persian and Arabic such a sinking bowl is called *pingan, fingǎn*, and *binkam*, the meaning of which extends from "bowl" or "cup" to "unit of time", or to a clepsydra in general. Two nineteenth-century orientalists, F. Justi and Th. Nöldeke, recognised in the word the Greek πίναξ [2]. The diminutive πινάκιον would correspond even better, especially as one of its meanings is "small plate or cup" [3]. In North Africa the bowl is called *qadas* from the Latin *cadus*, which in its turn is the Greek κάδος [4].

It has been said that in the seventeenth century the Dutch brought such sinking bowls from India to Persia. They did indeed present the Shah of Persia with *gory schotels* [5]. But the Hindi word (*ghari*) means both the floating cup and the gong which is struck to announce the time [6], and in our case it is much more likely that the present consisted of gongs.

3. ISLAMIC SUNDIALS

An incredible amount of ingenuity went into the construction of new sundials. References in Vitruvius (IX, 8) show that the Greeks produced a considerable number of books in which new types of sundial were worked out, but this is nothing compared to what Arabic authors wrote on the subject [7]. The nonmathematician can only admire their constructions from a re-

---

[1] E. Wiedemann & F. Hauser, 'Über die Uhren im Bereich der islamischen Kultur', *Abhandlungen der Kaiserl. Leop.-Carol. Deutschen Akad. d. Naturforscher*, Halle, 1915, pp. 20, 22 f., 165 f.

[2] L. Fleischer, 'Studien über Dozys Supplément', *Berichte d. K. Sächs. Gesellsch. d. Wiss.*, Leipzig, 38, 1886, 190-193. Th. Nöldeke, 'Persische Studien', *Sitzungsberichte Akad. d. Wiss. Wien*, 126, 1892, 12. Abh., 38. Nöldeke had already drawn attention to the occurrence of the word in Aramaic.

[3] Preisigke, *Wörterbuch d. griech. Papyrusurk.*, s.v.

[4] A. Mez, *Die Renaissance des Islams*, 1922, 428.

[5] Cornelis Spelman, *Journal der reiz van den gezant der O.I.Compagnie Joan Cunaeus naar Perzie in 1651-1652*, 1908, 146.

[6] Yule & Burnell, *Hobson-Jobson*, 1903, 372; s.v. Ghurry.

[7] K. Schoy, *Die Gnomonik der Araber*, 1923 (*Die Geschichte der Zeitmessung*, Bd. 1, Lief. F).

spectful distance without pretending to understand the highly involved details. On the other hand, the sundials in actual use were normally of a simple kind. Not everybody was a trained mathematician, but everybody had to say his prayers at certain hours.

Ernst Zinner, the historian of astronomy and of scientific instruments, has made the surprising claim that two sundials described by a thirteenth-century Arabic author from Morocco were German inventions. Abū'l-Ḥasan ʿAlī, in the eighties of the thirteenth century, wrote a book on astronomical instruments in which he described a shadow-clock consisting of a wooden board and a gnomon which has to be put into one of six sockets according to the position of the sun in the zodiac [1]. Zinner was of course fully aware that this sundial worked on the principle of the ancient Egyptian shadow-clock, but he thought it unlikely that the Egyptian tradition was then still alive, and preferred to think that it was an adaptation of the "Germanic suspended sundial with movable gnomon. And this becomes even more probable as the author also describes the column sundial, which is certainly a German invention" [2].

These two types of suspended sundial have much in common, or rather the second is only a slight modification of the first. The hour-scale is arranged in six vertical columns, each for two months equidistant from the equinox. The detachable gnomon is put into a socket on top of the scale which corresponds to the month in which one uses the sundial. Type I is flat, type II, the column sundial, is cylindrical.

What Zinner claimed to be the "Germanic" prototype of the Islamic type is represented by a single specimen, a small "Anglo-Saxon" sundial of silver which was found at Canterbury in 1939. It is always regarded as dating from the tenth century, or from

---

[1] Aboul Hhassan Ali, *Traité des instruments astronomiques*, trad. J.-J. Sédillot, II, 1835, 440 ff. On the author see Sarton, *Introduction to the History of Science*, II, 623.
[2] E. Zinner, *Deutsche und niederländische astronomische Instrumente*, 1956 (2. Aufl. 1967), 13.

the years around A.D. 1000 [1]. However, it seems to me that the style of lettering leaves no doubt that this sundial is of post-Conquest date. As for its Islamic counterpart, we have not only the description with a drawing of it in the thirteenth-century work, but also an actual specimen, now in the Bibliothèque Nationale in Paris, which was made in A.D. 1159 (554 A.H.) for the Zengid ruler Nūr-ad-dīn [2]. The similarity between the English and the Syrian sundials is very striking indeed [3], and there is a very simple explanation for it. Paul Casanova in his exemplary publication of Nūr-ad-dīn's sundial has already pointed out that it follows a Greco-Egyptian tradition.

The column sundial, which is according to Zinner "without doubt a German invention", was described for the first time in a short text which goes under the name of Hermannus Contractus, abbot of Reichenau (1013-1054) [4]. Zinner concluded from the absence of Arabic loan-words in the description that the invention itself could not be of Islamic origin [5]. But the description forms part of a group of short treatises, the purpose of which was to bring the achievements of Islamic science to the knowledge of Christian Europe.

We might say that the suspended flat sundial belonged to the classical tradition which lived on both in the East and the West, and that the suspended column sundial was an Islamic invention which reached the West in the eleventh century.

---

[1]   Only Needham (*SCC* III, 302 n.) dates it "ninth century". A report on the discovery appeared in *The Times*, July 31, 1939, p. 9.   Zinner, *l.c.*, 49.   Ward, *Descr. Cat.* (see above, p. 2 n. 2), No. 109.   Reproduced in E. v. Bassermann-Jordan and H. v. Bertele, *The Book of Clocks and Watches*, 1964, fig. 17.

[2]   P. Casanova, 'La montre du sultan Nour ad Din', *Syria*, 4, 1923, 282-299. E. Herzfeld, *Inscriptions et monuments d'Alep*, 1955, I/1, p. 232, No. 109bis. L. A. Mayer, *Islamic Astrolabists and Their Works*, 1956, 52 f.

[3]   Derek J. Price has already reproduced them side by side as being "strikingly similar", without going into the question of a genetic relationship (*A History of Technology*, III, 1957, 596).

[4]   *De utilitatibus astrolabii* II, 1 (*Patrologia Latina* 143, 405). It has been printed as being by Hermannus, but his authorship is more than doubtful; see J. M. Millás Vallicrosa, *Estudios sobre historia de la ciencia española*, 1949, 89, 121 (criticism of Zinner); *idem*, *Nuevos estudios*, 1960, 104.

[5]   In an earlier publication Zinner thought that Hermann's column sundial was "vermutlich gemäss einem arabischen Vorbilde entstanden" ('Horologium Viatorum', *Isis*, 14, 1930, 385-387).

4. ISLAMIC WATER-CLOCKS

In constructing elaborate water-clocks the Arabs were likewise the heirs and pupils of the Greeks. The water-clock is occasionally called *surrāqat al-mā*, "thief of water", a literal, one might say too literal, translation of the Greek word clepsydra [1].

The first Islamic clock to reach the West was a water-clock in the best Alexandrian tradition. The report on the embassy of Harun ar-Rashid which arrived at the court of Charlemagne in 807 has often been quoted, but it is still worth while to refer to it again [2]. The leader of the embassy was a Muhammadan, but he was accompanied by Christian monks from Jerusalem who evidently acted as interpreters. The envoys brought many gifts, among them a tent, precious silks, candlesticks of enormous size, but above all a water-clock made of brass. At the completed hour metal pellets fell on a kind of gong and produced a sound. At the same time twelve equestrian figures appeared through doors, which opened and closed mechanically.

These were amazing novelties in ninth-century Europe, but such clocks had already a long history in the East. A Greek treatise which goes under the name of Archimedes, and is preserved only in an Arabic translation, gives the description of such a clock with all these devices, like the falling and sound-producing metal pellets, the men on horseback, the doors which open and shut as if by magic, and in addition twittering birds and little figures of men making music [3].

We are apt to smile at these clocks as something childish, but

[1] Wiedemann-Hauser, *Uhren*, 7. On the Greek word which originally meant a kind of pipette, and not a clock, see H. Diels, *Antike Technik*, 2. Aufl. 1920, 192.

[2] Einhart, *Annales*, a. 807 (*Mon. Germ.*, *Scriptores*, I, 194; Schlosser, *Schriftquellen z. Gesch. d. karol. Kunst*, No. 68): "horologium ex auricalco arte mechanica mirifice compositum, in quo XII horarum cursus ad clepsidram vertebatur, cum totidem aereis pilulis quae ad completionem horarum decidebant et casu suo subiectum sibi cimbalum tinnire faciebant, additis in eodem eiusdem numeri equitibus, qui per XII fenestras completis horis exiebant, quae prius erant apertae claudebant. Nec non et alia multa erant in ipso horologio, quae nunc enumerare longum est".

[3] E. Wiedemann & F. Hauser, 'Uhr des Archimedes und zwei andere Vorrichtungen', *Nova Acta. Abhandlungen d. Kaiserl. Leop.-Carol. Deutschen Akad. d. Naturforscher*, 103, Halle 1918. A. E. Drachmann (*Ktesibios, Philon and Heron*, 1948, 36-41) thinks that the treatise is of Islamic origin.

who is so *blasé* that he never stopped in front of one of them, and waited for the figures, the "jacks", to go through their hourly exercises? In the fourteenth century, the first century of the mechanical clock, public clocks were already expected to do more than merely show the time. Very often they continued the traditional puppet-show of the old water-clocks, the only difference being that the motive power was no longer water, but the falling weights. A famous surviving example is the clock in Wells Cathedral where knights on horseback joust with each other at the stroke of the hour [1].

The achievements of Islamic technology, both in continuing the Greek tradition and in adding to it, can best be seen in the *Book of the Knowledge of Mechanical Devices* by al-Jazarī, an admirable work which can be studied in the annotated translation of Donald R. Hill [2]. Jazarī lived at that remarkable cultural centre, the court of the Artuqid rulers at Dyarbakir in what is now Eastern Turkey. He had spent some twenty-five years constructing all kinds of mechanical device, and especially ingenious and complicated water-clocks, when one day Sultan Nasīr ad-Din Mahmud (1200-1222) asked him to write down what he had achieved. He finished his treatise in A.D. 1206. It is not, like some of the later Western works of this type, a technological utopia, a collection of devices which seem to work only on paper, but a summary of the life-work of an extremely gifted engineer. In the introduction he tells us that he had studied, not without criticism, the existing literature on the subject, and that he had looked at what had been produced in that particular field. His various mechanisms are conceived in the spirit of Heron and the other Greeks, but they are not slavish imitations. It must be stressed that, unlike the Greeks, he gives detailed instructions on how to produce these devices, including the exact measurements of the single parts, the

---

[1] On the clock at Wells see R. P. Howgrave-Graham, 'Notes on the History of Horology', *Archaeologia*, 77, 1928, 293 ff.

[2] Al-Jazarī, *The Book of Knowledge of Ingenious Mechanical Devices*, translated and annotated by D. R. Hill, 1974. There exists an earlier German translation by Wiedemann-Hauser, *Uhren* (see above, p. 4 n. 1).

materials which are most suitable, and what must be observed in the process of construction. It is a "do-it-yourself" manual and a highly successful one; it was translated into Persian at an unknown date, probably early, and into Turkish in the sixteenth century. Of the Arabic original there exists a fine manuscript dating from the thirteenth century (in Istanbul)[1], several artistically remarkable ones from the Mamluk period, and a number of late copies, some of which date from the seventeenth century[2]. As we have excellent early manuscripts, it may seem pointless to stress the existence of these late copies, but we shall have to come back to them.

A page from a manuscript of the work copied in A.D. 1315 shows the "Elephant Clock" (Fig. 1)[3]. When the hour, or rather half-hour, strikes, one pair of eyes will not be sufficient: so much is happening at the same time. The bird on top begins to sing, the cupola turns, the man at the top left moves his arm, the falcon drops a metal pellet from his beak into the mouth of the upper dragon, the two dragons move, and the pellet finally lands in the small vase, the mahout moves his ankus and beats the drum on the elephant's head, while the scribe turns and indicates the hour on a scale.

In the treatise itself each picture is followed by a series of detailed working drawings, e.g. (Fig. 2) the turning figure of the scribe who indicates the hour with his calamus. These drawings also show the hidden parts of the mechanism[4].

[1] On this manuscript (Ahmet III, 3472) see E. Akurgal, C. Mango and R. Ettinghausen, *Treasures of Turkey*, 1966, 168 ff. (with a colour reproduction). An instructive juxtaposition of a miniature from this manuscript and a Mamluk copy can be found in F. Rosenthal, *Four Essays on Art and Literature in Islam*, 1971, pl. 2.

[2] On the manuscripts of the treatise see K. Holter, 'Die islamischen Miniaturhandschriften vor 1350', *Zentralblatt für Bibliothekswesen*, 54, 1937, 5-8 (and addenda in *Ars Islamica*, 7, 1940, 148 f.); E. J. Grube, *Islamic Paintings in the Collection of H. P. Kraus*, n.d., 50 ff. A late copy of the miniature with the Elephant Clock is in the Museum of Islamic Art at Cairo (No. 14, 017); see Bishr Farès, 'L'Horloge du Palais', *Bulletin de l'Institut d'Égypte*, 40, 1969, 7-9.

[3] Wiedemann-Hauser, *Uhren*, 116 ff. Single leaf from an al-Jazarī manuscript in the Metropolitan Museum of Art, New York (Cora Timken Burnett Bequest, 1956); discussed and reproduced in colour in R. Ettinghausen, *Arab Painting*, 1962, 93 ff.

[4] Wiedemann-Hauser, *Uhren*, 120 f. Single leaf from an al-Jazarī manuscript

In the thirteenth century again we hear of a remarkable clock which was brought from the Islamic East to Christian Europe; in all likelihood it was the last one to make the East-West journey. What the Sultan of Egypt (*Soldanus Babilonie*, Kāmil) sent in 1232 to the emperor Frederick II was not just a clock, but a combination of clock and planetarium. Inside a tent the planets moved and Sun and Moon indicated without fail (*infallibiter*) the time of the day or night. The chroniclers mention the gold and the jewels used for this *celum astronomicum*, and that it was worth more than 20,000 marks, but they are silent on the mechanism. Frederick II kept it at Venosa (Basilicata) among his treasures and regarded it as one of his most precious possessions [1].

5. The Use of Arab Astrolabes in Christian Europe

The Arabs always called the astrolabe by its Greek name, thereby acknowledging that it was an ingenious Greek idea to invent an instrument for astronomical observation and calculation which consists essentially of a simplified star map which can be made to rotate against the background of a stereographic projection of the celestial sphere [2]. The enormous popularity of the astrolabe in the East and the West is due to the fact that it can be used for a wide variety of purposes, ranging from astronomy to astrology and even including surveying. We think of an astrolabe as a scientific instrument, but it could equally well be described as a device for measuring time [3]. The astrolabe was not invented for that purpose, but in the Islamic East and later in the Christian West it was probably much more used for telling the time from

of A.H. 715 (A.D. 1315) in the L. A. Mayer Memorial, Jerusalem (ex Sotheby, December 7, 1970, lot 13).

[1]   *Chronica Regia Coloniensis*, cont. IV, a. 1232 (rec. Waitz, 1880, p. 263). Conrad de Faberia, *Casus S. Galli*, c. 14 (*Mon. Germ., Scriptores*, II, 178): "celum astronomicum aureum gemmis stellatum, habens philosophicum intra se cursum planetarum". E. Winckelmann (*Kaiser Friedrich II*, 1897, II, 399 n. 5) has argued that the planetarium was a gift from al-Ashraf. See also J. D. North, 'Opus quorundam rotarum mirabilium', *Physis*, 8, 1966, 364 ff.

[2]   O. Neugebauer, 'The Early History of the Astrolabe', *Isis*, 40, 1949, 240-256.

[3]   The earliest Latin description of the astrolabe (from the eleventh century) calls it a *horologium* (also *orologium regis Ptolomei*); see J. M. Millás Vallicrosa, *Nuevos estudios sobre historia de la ciencia española*, 1960, 95.

the altitude of the sun than for any other purpose. As an Arabic author said: "Our kings and scholars use in daytime an astrolabe and during the night a water-clock. In daytime they have in addition to the astrolabe the sundial also [1]".

Both Byzantium and Western Europe learned from the Arabs the use of this originally Greek instrument, and they seem to have taken their first lessons at more or less the same time. A Byzantine astrolabe of Islamic type dates from the eleventh century [2]. In Catalonia, a country geographically close to the Islamic world and the first to establish scientific contacts with it, the astrolabe was well known in the eleventh century [3]. Its enthusiastic reception in the Christian world was greatly helped by the fact that the calendar ring of the astrolabes from the Maghreb and the Near East showed the solar months, and even the Julian [4].

In the late Middle Ages, at a time when the West had already produced astrolabes of impeccable workmanship, there seems to have existed a feeling that the Islamic variety was preferable and of superior quality. A surprisingly high percentage of the early Islamic astrolabes show by their added Latin inscriptions that they must have reached the West during the Middle Ages. As the majority came from Spain, we should avoid speaking of an East-West journey and rather say that they travelled from the Muhammadan to the Christian world. To use an Oriental instrument would have presented no particular problem to a Westerner

[1] E. Wiedemann, *Beiträge* X, *Sitzungsberichte d. phys.-med. Sozietät in Erlangen*, 38, 1906, 348.

[2] On the Byzantine astrolabe of 1062 see O. M. Dalton, 'The Byzantine Astrolabe at Brescia', *Proceedings of the British Academy*, 1926, 133-146, and the important remarks of O. Neugebauer, *Isis*, 40, 1949, 249.

[3] J. M. Millás Vallicrosa, *Assaig d'història de les idees físiques i matemàtiques a la Catalunya medieval*, 1931. Millás studied also the Arabic treatises and their translations: 'Los primeros tratados de astrolabio en la España árabe', a chapter in his *Nuevos estudios sobre historia de la ciencia española*, 1960, 61-78.

[4] "Spanish-Moorish astrolabes always have a Julian calendar, Egyptian, a Julian or Coptic, while Persian never have any solar calendar" (W. Hartner, 'Asturlab', *Encyclopaedia of Islam*, 2nd. ed., II, 726; reprinted in his collected papers *Oriens-Occidens*, 1968, 316). Millás has argued that the circle of months was an Islamic invention and did not exist on the original Greek astrolabes (*Estudios sobre historia de la ciencia española*, 1949, 114).

who knew how to handle an astrolabe, and that meant at the time every educated person. The scales and gradations were the same, and adding the Latin names of the months and of signs of the zodiac to enable a quick orientation was easy enough.

Occasionally an early astrolabe reached the Christian world only centuries after it was made [1]. Such a one, made by Aḥmad ibn Muḥammad at Saragossa in A.H. 472 (A.D. 1079/80) has the Latin names of the months engraved in classical capital letters which can hardly antedate the Renaissance [2]. The re-engraving was evidently done in Italy [3]. Instead of the names of the signs of the zodiac the engraver used the symbols in their modern form, as they were familiar to him from calendars. This is an instance of an early Islamic instrument used by a Renaissance astronomer.

A practically contemporary astrolabe, also from Islamic Spain, this time from Toledo, was made there in A.H. 460 (A.D. 1068) by Ibrahim ibn Saʿīd, just seventeen years before the Christian *reconquista* of the town [4]. Here the Latin inscriptions are considerably earlier, although not contemporary with the astrolabe itself; they seem to date from the thirteenth or fourteenth century. The conventional symbols of the zodiacal signs look more archaic than on the astrolabe from Saragossa [5].

A number of such astrolabes exists, with added Latin inscriptions from Islamic Spain and North Africa. Our knowledge of the

---

[1]   Mediaeval astronomers were aware that in using an old astrolabe one had to take into consideration the changes due to the precession of the equinoxes (Millás Vallicrosa, *Estudios*, etc. 342, 344). Whether this was always observed is a different matter.

[2]   Germanisches Museum, Nuremberg (W.J. 353). L. A. Mayer, *Islamic Astrolabists and their Works*, 1956, 37, pl. 3.

[3]   The month of July appears abbreviated as LV, a solecism in a Latin text which is only explicable if we assume that the craftsman was an Italian who fell into his native idiom (*luglio*).

[4]   Museum of the History of Science, Oxford. Reproduced in R. T. Gunther, *The Astrolabes of the World*, 1932, No. 118, pl. 60. Mayer, *l.c.*, 51, No. II.

[5]   As on all astrolabes from Islamic Spain the original inscriptions give the names of the Julian months, i.e. their Latin names in Arabic transcriptions. Gunther, *l.c.*, 256, quotes Professor Margoliouth in saying that the Latin-Arabic names of the months on the Toledo astrolabe indicate "an Italian rather than a Spanish source". As the names are the usual ones it is difficult to see what could be Italian about them. Exactly the same transcriptions are found in the Calendar of Cordova (R. Dozy and Ch. Pellat, *Le Calendrier de Cordove*, 1961, 25 ff.) and elsewhere.

development of Gothic epigraphic script is still so imperfect that it is not possible to date the inscriptions exactly, but one can safely state that they can hardly be very much later than the astrolabes themselves. As examples one could quote an astrolabe signed by 'Uthmān ibn 'Abdallah at Fez in A.D. 1299 [1], or one by Aḥmad ibn Ḥusain ibn Bāṣo of Granada, of A.D. 1309 [2].

Not all the astrolabes which reached the Christian world in the Middle Ages came from the Maghreb. Two remarkable examples, and from the artistic point of view perhaps the finest astrolabes in existence, were produced in the thirteenth century, one certainly, the other very likely, in Egypt. They are the only astrolabes where the rete is decorated with figures of animals and human beings, but it would be wrong to assume that this was a concession to the artistic taste of non-Muhammadans. The first is signed by 'Abd al-Karīm. The style of the Latin inscriptions shows that it was in the hands of a Christian soon after it was made, but he could not have been its first owner. A curious alteration in the Arabic text, which was spotted by the late L. A. Mayer, makes it evident that it had remained in Muhammadan hands during the first years of its existence [3]. Very similar in style is an astrolabe, now at Nuremberg, which is signed by As-Sahl the Astrolabist (Fig. 3) [4]. It is believed to have belonged to the great astronomer Regiomontanus (1436-1476). His ownership is not absolutely certain, but very

---

[1]   Museo di Storia della Scienza, Florence. Mayer, *l.c.*, 84, pl. 4b.

[2]   Private collection, Paris. Mayer, *l.c.*, 17, 36, No. III, pl. 7. In the Latin inscriptions the month of May is called MADI[us], a spelling found on other astrolabes too, and said to point to Italian origin (*Supplement to a Catalogue of Scientific Instruments in the Collection of J. A. Billmeir*, Oxford 1957, 32). Madius is a common mediaeval spelling; the dictionaries (e.g. *Novum glossarium mediae Latinitatis*, 1957, s.v.) register examples from France and elsewhere; see also the sceptical attitude of B. Migliorini quoted in *Physis*, 12, 1970, 87.

[3]   British Museum. D. Barrett, *Islamic Metalwork in the British Museum*, 1949, pls. 19-20. Mayer, *l.c.*, 30.

[4]   The property of the Stadtbibliothek, but on loan to the Germanisches Museum (W.J. 20). The astrolabe is not dated; the *Répertoire chronologique d'épigraphie arabe* (XIII, No. 5066) lists it with unwarranted preciseness under the year H. 698. Mayer (*l.c.*, 82) more cautiously dated it before H. 698/A.D. 1299, as it was made for al-Malik al-Muẓaffar Taqiaddīn who has been identified with an Ayyubid ruler of Hama who died in that year. But as we find at Hama two earlier Ayyubids with this name not even that date can be regarded as certain.

likely [1]. Here we find no re-engraving, but instead an added plate to make the astrolabe usable in the Northern world. The plate (Fig. 3b) has been marked in typically fifteenth-century German script "L[atitudo] 48", which is the latitude of Nuremberg.

The adding of plates specially computed for the town where the owner lived was common practice. A contemporary of Regiomontanus, Martin Bylica (1433-1495), court astrologer to King Mathias Corvinus of Hungary, used a Moorish astrolabe which had been made in Cordoba in A.D. 1054. He had it re-engraved and added plates for Padua and Buda [2].

In the cases mentioned—the list could easily be extended—the added Latin inscriptions are confined to the circles of the months and of the zodiac. The owners of the astrolabes did not bother to have the star names on the rete translated, evidently thinking that they were of no great practical use for time-measuring. On Islamic astrolabes the degrees are always indicated not by the new Hindu numerals, but by the traditional letters of the Arabic alphabet. Here again re-engraving was not considered necessary as one could always identify the degree in question by simple counting.

One learns, however, with some surprise that adding Latin inscriptions to an Islamic astrolabe was standard practice almost from the very moment the West learned about the existence of this instrument. An eleventh-century manuscript of a Latin treatise on the astrolabe is adorned with two remarkable drawings of the front and back of such an instrument. The draughtsman depicted an Arabic astrolabe, the inscriptions on which (including the signature of the maker) were carefully copied by somebody who had a thorough training in Arabic calligraphy. To these were

[1]   E. Zinner, *Leben und Wirken des J. Müller von Königsberg genannt Regiomontanus*, 1938, 167. I am purposely quoting the first edition of this book, and not the second revised one of 1968, because there the astrolabe is confused with the other Arabic one in the Museum at Nuremberg (see above, p., 12). See also E. Zinner, 'Wissenschaftliche Instrumente', in *Keysers Kunst- und Antiquitätenbuch*, II, 1959, 76.
[2]   The astrolabe, now at Cracow, formed part of the Polish loans to the Copernicus exhibition which in 1973 was shown in a number of countries. K. Estreicher, *Collegium maius*, 1967, fig. 38. *Nicolas Copernic ou La révolution astronomique*, Bibliothèque Nationale, Paris 1973, No. 170.

added in Latin the names of the signs of the zodiac from Aries to Pisces and the months from January to December (Fig. 4) [1].

Were bilingual astrolabes ever produced for export to the Christian world? There exists no real evidence to assume it. As we have seen some of the astrolabes were re-engraved considerably later, and of the one from Egypt we know that it was originally made for a Muhammadan patron. Still, in the majority of cases the re-engraving seems to have been done soon after the instrument was made, and one could easily imagine that among the mixed population of Spain it was occasionally done on the spot.

It is worth mentioning that the practice of re-engraving and using an Islamic astrolabe was not restricted to Christians. An astrolabe signed by Muhammad b. aṣ-Ṣaffār in Toledo in A.D. 1029 shows added Hebrew inscriptions of exactly the same type: the names of the constellations of the zodiac, and the Latin names of the months in Hebrew transcription [2].

The quadrant is a reduced and handy version of the astrolabe. The historians of scientific instruments will object to this definition, on the ground that only at a later stage of its development, with the invention of the *quadrans novus* by Profeit Tibbon, at the end of the thirteenth century, did it take over the stereographic network of the astrolabe. It remains, however, a fact that its earliest Western description, dating from the eleventh century, already called it *orologium cum astrolabii quarta parte*, a quarter of an astrolabe [3]. Like the astrolabe it could be used for many purposes,

---

[1]   Paris, Bibliothèque Nationale, Ms. lat. 7412. The drawings were first published by A. van den Vyver, 'Les premiers traductions latins (Xe-XIe s.) des traités arabes sur l'astrolabe', *Ier Congrès International de Géographie Historique*, Bruxelles 1931. On this manuscript see also M. Destombes, 'Un astrolabe carolingien et l'origine de nos chiffres arabes', *Archives Internationales d'Histoire des Sciences*, 15, 1962, 25; P. Kunitzsch, *Arabische Sternnamen in Europa*, 1959, 90 ff.

[2]   Staatsbibliothek, Berlin. The front is reproduced in T. Mann, *Der Islam einst und jetzt*, 1914, fig. 48, the back in Mayer, *l.c.*, pl. 2.

[3]   The fundamental study of the early history of the quadrant is J. M. Millás Vallicrosa, 'La introducción del cuadrante con cursor en Europa', *Isis*, 17, 1932, 218-258; reprinted in his *Estudios sobre historia de la ciencia española*, 1949, 65-110. In these publications Millás dated cod. Ripoll 225 "tenth century", but corrected it later to "eleventh century" (*Gesammelte Aufsätze zur Kulturgeschichte Spaniens*, 26, 1971, p. 147, n. 120).

but was most often consulted as an *orologium* to tell the time. The Christian world learned about its use through translations of Arabic books, but there is no evidence that actual Islamic quadrants were ever used outside their homeland.

6. Epilogue: The Phase of Peaceful Collaboration (Sicily and Spain)

The period of European supremacy was preceded by a phase of peaceful meeting of the two civilisations. The historian who wants to study cultural contacts between East and West will always have to turn to Sicily and to Spain in the twelfth and thirteenth centuries. In both cases we have to deal with a trilingual civilisation, Arabic-Greek-Latin in Sicily, Arabic-Hebrew-Latin in Spain.

At Palermo, in the Royal Palace, outside the Cappella Palatina, can still be seen an inscription in three languages set up by King Roger II in 1142 to celebrate the erection of a clock. The clock itself has long disappeared. The inscription, which a modern author aptly described as "in terse Latin, fulsome Greek, and flowery Arabic"; makes it clear that this clock must have been something extraordinary [1].

The thirteenth century in Spain was, as far as clock-making is concerned, an exciting period of experiment. A cleverly devised alarm-clock is described in an unexpected place, the *Zohar*, the sacred book of Jewish mysticism. The *Zohar* purports to date from the second century of our era, but it became known only in the second half of the thirteenth century. When it turned up unexpectedly it was rumoured at once that Moses de Leon (d. 1305) was in reality its author. Recent scholarship, especially the investigations of Gershom Scholem, has shown that the language

---

[1] Cecilia Waern, *Mediaeval Sicily*, 1910, 46. An engraving of the inscription can be found in S. Morso, *Descrizione di Palermo antico*, 2a ed., 1827, pl. 3. M. Amari, *Le epigrafe arabiche di Sicilia*, a cura di F. Gabrieli, 1971, 29-39. Amari has tried to connect the inscription with a poetical reference to a water-clock constructed by a Maltese mathematician where the figure of a girl dropped metal pellets into a resounding basin. *Répertoire chronol. d'épigraphie arabe*, VIII, No. 3106.

of the *Zohar* is not genuinely ancient, but pseudo-archaic, and that the author gives himself away by locutions which belong to the usage of his own day [1]. The cultural historian who is unable to follow these esoteric philological paths is struck by amazing anachronisms in the book. The rearing of silkworms, for example, was unknown in second-century Palestine [2].

The passage which interests us here reads in translation: "Rabbi Abba set out from Tiberias to go to the house of his father-in-law. With him was his son Rabbi Jacob. When they arrived at Kfar Tarsha, they stopped to spend the night. Rabbi Abba inquired of his host: Have you a cock there? The host said: Why? Said Rabbi Abba: I wish to rise exactly at midnight. The host replied: A cock is not needed. I have in my house a device (to announce midnight). By my bed there is a scale (with a clepsydra hanging from one side which) I fill with water. It drips out drop by drop, until just at midnight it is all out, and then this weight moves, and produces a sound which is audible in the whole house, and then it is exactly midnight. This clock I made for a certain old man who was in the habit of getting up each night at midnight to study Torah. To this Rabbi Abba said: Blessed be God for guiding me here" [3].

J. D. Eisenstein [4] has published a convincing reconstruction of this mechanism (Fig. 5). The water-clock is fixed to a steelyard. As soon as the water-vessel is empty, one arm of the steelyard will jerk up, while the one with the container will come down with a

---

[1] G. Scholem, *Major Trends in Jewish Mysticism*, 1961, 156 ff.; the same, 'Zohar', *Encyclopaedia Judaica*, 16, 1971, 1193-1215.

[2] G. Scholem, *Die Geheimnisse der Schöpfung. Ein Kapitel aus dem Sohar*, 1935, 45. The author of the *Zohar* was neither the only nor the first person to project silk-production back into classical antiquity. The family of the Spanish scholar Isaac ben Baruch (eleventh century) traced its origin back to Jewish silk-weavers which Titus had sent to Spain after the capture of Jerusalem (H. Lewy, *Journal of the Warburg Institute*, 1, 1938, 253).

[3] *Zohar* 92a. English translation in *Zohar. The Book of Splendour*, selected and edited by G. G. Scholem, 1949, 45. I am deeply grateful to Gershom Scholem for having provided me with a more literal translation of this passage specially made for the purposes of this book, and with notes on the various readings and the philological problems involved. The translation quoted above is this literal one.

[4] *The Jewish Encyclopaedia*, 6, 464.

bang and sound the alarm. A similar mechanism was described by a twelfth-century Arabic author: there the vessel is gradually getting emptier, i.e. lighter, and a scale on the steelyard shows, instead of the weight, the hour [1]. In the *Zohar* the constant weighing has been replaced by a simple alarm. It is a new twist given to the Arabic device, which in its turn was the adaptation of a Chinese invention [2]; an instructive example of how such knowledge travelled from civilisation to civilisation, and finally reached the West.

Of much greater historical importance is the mercury clock invented by a Jew, Rabbi Isaac ibn Sid, and described by King Alfonso el Sabio (1252-82) in his *Libros del saber de astronomía* [3]. The clock, famous in the history of horology, is driven by a weight fixed to a drum. The drum itself is divided into twelve compartments or chambers. Six of them are filled with mercury, and all twelve communicate by means of holes in the walls. The weight would come down at once were it not for the heavy quicksilver which moves slowly from one compartment to another and acts as an escapement, enabling the clock to keep time. The mercury clock had no future and was soon replaced by the clock with a verge-and-foliot escapement, but a new principle had been discovered, the regulating escapement.

To say that the mercury clock had no future is perhaps slightly exaggerated. The idea of the chambers with percolating quicksilver was taken up in the early fifteenth century by that *homme à*

---

[1] On al-Khazini's steelyard clepsydra s. E. Wiedemann, *Beiträge* XXXVII: 'Über die Stundenwage', *Sitzungsberichte d. phys.-med. Soz. Erlangen*, 46, 1914, 27 ff. and Wiedemann-Hauser, *Uhren*, 30.

[2] J. Needham, *Science and Civilisation in China*, I, 204; III, 318, 326-328; IV/2, 480, 499n. As Needham has pointed out the Chinese had been using such steelyard clepsydras for centuries when in the tenth century they heard about an identical device on one of the gates of the capital of Fulin (Rome). The clepsydra was combined with the golden figure of a man and golden balls which fell to indicate the hours. The Chinese texts have been translated by F. Hirth, *China and the Roman Orient*, 1885, 53, 57, 213. Hirth and the majority of scholars identified the capital of Fulin with Antioch; C. P. Fitzgerald decided for Constantinople (*China. A Short Cultural History*, 1935, 323, followed by J. Beckwith, *Early Christian and Byzantine Art*, 1970, 80).

[3] Alfonso X, *Libros del saber de astronomía*, com. M. Rico y Sinoras, 1866, IV, 65 ff. G. Bilfinger, *Die mittelalterlichen Horen und die modernen Stunden*, 1892, 153.

projets, Giovanni Fontana [1]. From time to time, long after the mechanical clock had become universal, the old idea was revived and clocks were built on the system of Alfonso el Sabio's, thereby showing that the idea was workable. Naturally these clocks remained curiosities [2].

[1] "Si rota cum argento vivo et capsulis intraperforatis superponatur, successive descendit per illam, quod pulcerrimum est". F. D. Prager, 'Fontana on Fountains, Venetian Hydraulics of 1418', *Physis*, 13, 1971, 345.

[2] On the history of these clocks see a fascinating paper by S. A. Bedini, 'The Compartmented Cylindrical Clepsydra', *Technology and Culture*, 3, 1962, 115-141. See also Needham, *l.c.*, III, 329 on a mechanical doll which a Dutch eighteenth-century author claimed to be a Chinese invention; *ibid.*, IV/2, 539 f. on Indian descriptions of a perpetual-motion machine of noria-type and filled with mercury. The idea of using mercury for the movement of automata figures is of classical origin; cf. Aristotle, *De anima*, I, 3.

CHAPTER I

THE SIXTEENTH CENTURY

1. Prelude: Mehmet II

The fourteenth and fifteenth centuries were the heroic age of horology. Innumerable improvements have been made since, but even to-day in the age of the atomic clock the majority of our clocks and watches run on the principles then evolved. About 1300 the mechanical clock was invented, with its combination of weight-driven power and regulating escapement. The new invention was taken up at once everywhere. Cathedrals, churches, palaces had to have such a clock, and it became a matter of civic pride to possess one superior to all others, not a mere utilitarian model to tell the hour, but one to indicate also the date, the day of the week, the sign of the zodiac, the age of the moon, and whatever else was, or might become, useful. In addition, the mechanical puppet theatre of the water-clocks was taken over—all these human figures, beasts and birds which make their appearance to announce the completed hour.

For over two hundred years nobody in the East showed the slightest interest in these new inventions [1]. The only exception is, characteristically, Mehmet II, the conqueror of Constantinople. Our information comes from Fra Francesco Suriano (1450-c. 1529), who in 1524 published a book on the Holy Land [2]. There

---

[1] In 1338 a Venetian merchant took a clock (*unum relogium*) to Delhi. C. M. Cipolla has drawn far-reaching conclusions from this fact (*Clocks and Culture 1300-1700*, 1967, preface): "That was a fateful event. Europe had begun to export machinery to Asia". Our information is extremely meagre, but it seems much more likely that the clock served as an aid in navigation; in that case it would have been an *orloge de mer*, i.e. a sand-glass.

[2] Francesco Suriano, *Il Trattato di Terra Santa e dell'Oriente*, edito da G. Golubovich, 1900, 94: "Quando la Signoria fece pace con lui del mille quatrocento settanta sette, pregòlla che li mandasse uno, che li facesse christallini, un'altro che li facesse horioli da sonare, e uno bono dipintore. Foli mandato maestro Zambellino (follows the story of a Madonna picture painted for the Sultan). Tuto questo, me presente, recontò questo maestro Zambellino, quando ritornò ad Venetia". Fra Francesco

he says that, after the peace treaty of 1477, Mehmet II asked the Signoria of Venice to send him somebody able to make *christallini* [1], somebody who could make striking clocks, and a good painter. The painter in question was Giovanni Bellini, who received the unexpected order to paint a Madonna for the Sultan [2]. "All this Master Giovanni Bellini related, in my presence, after his return to Venice."

If we could put our friar into the witness box, he would quickly break down under cross-examination. "You said that you heard all this from Giovanni Bellini himself who told you also about a picture which he had painted in Constantinople?" "That is correct". "May I point out to you that Giovanni Bellini never set foot in Constantinople, and that it was Gentile Bellini who went to Turkey, and that your whole story is therefore a pack of lies?" In spite of this contradiction, I believe that the worthy friar committed no worse crime than confusing the first names of the two Bellini brothers, who were both painters. That means that we can trust the incidental information contained in his report, namely that in the year 1477 at the instigation of Mehmet II for the first time a Western clockmaker went to Turkey.

Suriano, *Treatise of the Holy Land*, transl. by Th. Bellorini and E. Hoade, 1949, 107. The passage is not found in the manuscripts of the work, only in the printed edition of 1524. Uriel Heyd believed that Fra Francesco Suriano got the information from another Franciscan, Fra Bernardino da Foligno (*Zeitschrift der Deutschen Morgenländ. Gesellschaft*, 107, 1957, 655), but this seems most unlikely (F. Babinger, *Aufsätze und Abhandlungen*, I, 1962, 215).

[1] "che li facesse christallini". Hoade translated "one who made crystals", Babinger "ein Kristallschleifer (aus Murano)" (*Denkschriften Akad. Wiss. Wien*, 77, 1959, 16, n. 54). The guild regulations were strict in distinguishing between *cristalleri*, who worked in rock-crystal, on the one hand, and glass-blowers on the other. See G. Fiocco, 'A proposito di occhiali e di cristalli', *Arte Veneta*, 10, 1956, 213-214. I would regard it as likely that what Sultan Mehmet wanted was an expert craftsman able to grind spectacles. Eyeglasses had been invented in the West at about the same time as the mechanical clock; as with clocks it took a fairly long time for the new invention to be accepted in the East. In 1532 the Turkish *Defterdar* asked the Venetian *bailo* for a pair of spectacles, and got some of crystal mounted in silver (M. Sanudo, *I diarii*, 56, 402).

[2] The Sultan already possessed a Madonna in the Byzantine style (*grece*) and Bellini painted for him another *ala moderna*. The story of the Sultan's Madonna *Graecanico ritu depictam* has also been told by Francesco Negro who likewise had it from Gentile Bellini himself ("ex Gentili Bellino, mirabili Venetorum pictore, memini me audivisse"; G. Mercati, *Ultimi contributi alla storia degli umanisti*, II, 1939, 39*).

2. Süleyman I

Mehmet's third successor, Süleyman I, was also a great patron of the arts. Europeans called him "the Magnificent". His love for precious *objets d'art* was a godsend for the craftsmen of Venice who could always hope that an outstanding piece would tempt him to buy it. On October 2, 1531 Marino Sanudo saw at Venice a gold ring with a watch in it. In spite of its minute size the watch was in perfect working order, showed the time and struck the hours. It was intended to be sold in Turkey[1]. It was indeed bought by the Sultan as we learn from a letter by Pietro Aretino in which he mentions that the watchmaker was Giorgio (Capobianco) of Vicenza, who also produced a clockwork ship which served as a table decoration, and a mechanical doll which could dance. Aretino was not impressed: "These things are amusements for women"[2]. A watch of such minute size was obviously something unheard of at the time[3]. It may have been the first, but it was certainly not the last watch in a ring. Through the centuries many watchmakers have successfully competed with Giorgio Capobianco[4].

The next timepiece to reach Sultan Süleyman was of quite different dimensions. Twelve men were necessary to carry it into the audience chamber. The year was 1541. The Turks had just conquered the capital of Hungary. For King Ferdinand the situation was desperate and could only be saved by concluding a peace

[1] M. Sanudo, *I diarii*, 55, 14: "uno anello d'oro, sopra il qual è uno horologio bellissimo, qual lavora, dimostra le ore e sona, et quello (the son of the Venetian *bailo* in Constantinople) vol mandar a vender a Costantinopoli". This seems to be the "horologio picolo che lavora senza fermar" mentioned *ibid.* 56, 7, although one cannot be certain as one word (presumably *anello*) is missing in the text.

[2] Pietro Aretino, *Il primo libro delle lettere*, a cura di F. Nicolini, 1913, 369. Sanudo, *l.c.*, 55, 636 (on the "puta de legno qual con certa arte camina").

[3] As early as 1518 King Francis I of France bought from a watchmaker in Blois two daggers with watches in their hilts (G. H. Baillie, *Clocks and Watches. A Historical Bibliography*, 1951, 6). Rings with watches from the second half of the sixteenth century exist in various collections (E. Bassermann-Jordan, *Die Geschichte der Räderuhr*, 1905, 33; H. Thoma, *Schatzkammer der Residenz, München*, 1958, No. 590; E. Zinner, 'Die Augsburger Uhrmacherei von 1550 bis 1650', *Neue Uhrmacherzeitung*, Jg. 12, Heft 16, 1958, 29, figs. 9-11).

[4] At the Paris World Exhibition of 1900 Paul Ditisheim showed a watch which measured only 6.75 mm. It is of some interest in our context that it was bought by the Sultan of Morocco (W. I. Milham, *Time and Timekeepers*, 1913, 431 f., fig. 293; E. Jaquet and A. Chapuis, *Technique and History of the Swiss Watch*, 1953, 186).

treaty. The first thing was to please the Sultan so that he would receive the Austrian ambassadors. The gifts which they brought along in September 1541 were a golden and jewelled goblet and a machine of silver which combined a clock with a planetarium [1]. Not only did it indicate the hours: a complicated mechanism of cog-wheels and weights showed the movements of the sun, the moon and all the planets. It was said to have been made for the Emperor Maximilian I, who had spared no money to achieve perfection [2]. With the embassy came also the man who had constructed the planetarium, and left behind written instructions on how to repair it whenever this should become necessary [3].

Some three hundred years earlier a planetarium had travelled in the opposite direction as a gift from the Sultan to the emperor. Its memory was by then forgotten. What mattered was that Süleyman was highly pleased with the princely gift [4]. From now on a mission to the Sultan was unthinkable without presenting some outstanding clock. And, we may add, with the mission

[1] Described by Paolo Giovio who wrote almost immediately after the event, *Historiarum sui temporis libri*, 1577, 459 f.: "Tulere argenteam machinam, in qua non horarum modo specia: sed errantium etiam syderum motus, menstruique Solis ac Lunae coitus, exactissima ratione monstrabantur: intus scilicet dentatis rotis certisque ponderibus, admirabili momento, vel in multum aevum minutissimas temporum mensuras dispensantibus, quum inter celeres tardosque orbes, in tam vario inaequalique polorum ordine audaci quadam supremi motoris aemulatione cuncta congruerent. Ea a peritissimis astronomis excogitata, perfectaque Maximiliani Caesaris fuisse dicebatur, cuius ingenium nobili semper studio, nec deterrente unquam sumptu, rara atque admiranda concupivit".

[2] The contemporaneous description by Paolo Giovio leaves no doubt that it was a mechanical clock. G. H. Baillie (*Clocks and Watches. An Historical Bibliography*, 1951, 24) is mistaken in calling it a "waterclock". There seem to be no references to it from the time of Maximilian I unless we assume that it is identical with the *Theoria planetarum*, on which a number of craftsmen and scholars at Nuremberg worked (J. Neudörfer, *Nachrichten von Künstlern und Werkleuten*, hrsg. v. G. W. K. Lochner, 1875, pp. 66, 71).

[3] Giovio (*l.c.*) says: "Adduxerunt artificem qui solutis machinae fibulis interiora admirabili rotatione circumacta repanderet: is libellum quoque detulerat, attritae vel luxatae machinae remedia continentem, tradentemque praecepta, quibus tot orbium cursus numquam interitura ratione regeretur".

[4] Giovio (*l.c.*) stresses the Sultan's interest in astronomy and cosmography, and the instruction he got from his Jewish physician Hamon. On the latter see U. Heyd, 'Moses Hamon, Chief Physician to Sultan Süleyman the Magnificent', *Oriens*, 16, 1963, 152-170.

there always went from now on a clockmaker. Transporting these complicated and delicate mechanisms was a dangerous undertaking and what ambassador would have dared to appear at the Sublime Porte with a clock which refused to function?

3. FRANCE

With a new and startling clock you could gain the favour of the Sultan. The first to take the hint were the French [1]. In 1547 the king of France sent Sultan Süleyman a magnificent clock which served also as a table fountain. It had been made at Lyons and was rumoured to have cost the king 15,000 ducats [2].

Now at last the problem of what to give to the man who has everything had been solved. We are in the age of European expansion. Wherever Europeans appeared at the court of a foreign ruler in the Middle or the Far East, they ingratiated themselves by presenting one of these marvels of Western technology [3].

Receiving clocks and watches did not remain a privilege of the Sultan. The local rulers and officials expected these new instruments, together with the traditional gifts of precious textiles [4].

---

[1] Strictly speaking, the first Turk to receive a clock (*une horloge à mappemonde*) as a gift from the King of France was the famous admiral Barbaros Hayreddin in 1543/44 when the Turkish fleet wintered in Toulon (Ch. de La Roncière, *Histoire de la marine française*, 3, 1906, 387). An even earlier instance of a clock as a diplomatic gift is the *relogio* the Signoria of Venice sent in 1514 as a gift for the Mamluk Sultan Qansuh al-Ghuri. It never reached the Sultan as the Venetian consul in Alexandria thought it wiser to give it to the Sultan's chief interpreter (M. Sanudo, *I diarii*, 20, 168).

[2] Jean Chesneau, *Le voyage de Monsieur d'Aramon ambassadeur pour le roy en Levant*, publié et annoté par Ch. Schefer, 1887, pp. 17, 202: "un grand orloge faict à Lyon où y avoit une fontaine qui tiroit par l'espace de douze heures de l'eau qu'on y mettoit, qui estoit un chef d'œuvre et de hault pris". This was apparently not a mechanical clock, but one of those clepsydras which served also as table fountains and which then became fashionable in the seventeenth century.

[3] One of the first, if not the first, was Saint Francis Xavier who in 1551 presented the ruler at Yagamuchi with a "large, ingenious clock", a flintlock rifle with three barrels, eyeglasses, and other carefully selected objects which were unknown to the Japanese and duly impressed them (Luis Frois, *Die Geschichte Japans (1549-1578)*, übers. u. komment. v. G. Schurhammer u. E. A. Voretzsch, 1926, 14).

[4] "The next day the [French] Ambassador sent his presents unto the Basha [of Tripoli, in 1551], which were two fine peeces of Scarlet of Paris, one peece of fine Holland cloth, and one small clocke or dyall, which he received with very great contentment and pleasure". N. de Nicolay, *The Navigations into Turkey*, 1576, 19v.

Süleyman himself was insatiable in his demands. The diplomats at his court were set the task of providing watches more quickly than they could be manufactured. In 1558 the French ambassador in Constantinople had to write to his colleague in Venice [1]: "Je vous supplie mettre un mot dans vos lettres que S.M. m'envoye le plus que l'on pourra trouver de petites monstres, mesmement de celles qui sont avec sonnerie, pour le G[rand] S[eigneur], qui m'en a faict demander deux ou trois foys, estant entré despuis peu de temps en ça en ceste humeur d'en porter dix ou douze sur luy allant à la chasse. Ce qu'ayant entendu le bayle des Venitiens a faict expréssement une dépesche à la seigneurie pour en envoyer recouvrer à Paris, car S.H. n'en veult poinct d'aultres". In his reply the French king wrote from Fontainebleau on March 3, 1558 [2]: "Je vous envoye sept petites monstres d'horloge dont vous ferez present au G[rand] S[eigneur], et quelques-unes au bassa, en attendant que j'en envoye d'autres de ce mesme calibre, plus belles, mieux estoffées et sonnantes; mais il va beaucoup de temps a les faire, et ne s'en est peu trouver davantage que les sept, ayant à les vous envoyer ainsi promptement".

In spite of their feverish activity in procuring watches the French did not earn any gratitude. The Grand Vizier complained in 1563 that even the most humble person from Chios, Ragusa, Wallachia or Moldavia would not come to the Porte with empty hands. It was not the value of the gift which counted, but the honour rendered thus to the Sultan. Only the French were constantly making demands "sans toutesfois apporter un seul petit présent, fust'il d'une orloge ou d'un panier de fruict" [3].

Such remarks should never be taken literally, but that is exactly what the French did when in 1583 the circumcision of the Sultan's son was celebrated with fantastic pomp: they came along with a watch. The Venetian ambassador reported home to the Doge and Senate: "The Sultan was ill pleased with him [the

[1] E. Charrière, *Négociations de la France dans le Levant*, II, 1850, 432 n.
[2] *Ibid.*, 444 n.
[3] *Ibid.*, 718 n.

French ambassador] and his King, for on the occasion of the festival for the Sultan's son, while all other princes had made suitable presents, the King of France, who claimed to be so great a sovereign, had sent a watch only; at which the Sultan was very indignant and took it rather as a mark of contempt than of friendship" [1].

Some years earlier François de Noailles proudly told Charles IX how little he had paid for the clock which he gave to the Sultan: [2] "le grand horloge que j'avois acheté de vostre orfebvre à Paris, lequel a esté estimé dans le serail dix mil ducatz, et toutesfois ledit horloge avecque quelques autres bagateles que j'ay eues de luy, ne m'avoient cousté que deux mil livres et cinq cens escus. J'ay donné à Mehemet, premier bassa, de vostre part ... robes ... avecques un bel horloge". He ends his letter, addressing himself to the Queen-Mother: "Ayant sceu le premier bassa que j'avois un grand orloge pour présenter au G[rand] S[eigneur] de la part du roy, il m'envoia prier de luy envoier pour le veoir en sa maison, et, après l'avoir veu, me pria de luy en faire porter un pareil de France. Et pour ce, madame, que cela surmonte par trop mes forces, et que peut-estre il ne s'en pourroit plus retrouver de semblables, je me suis ressouvenu d'en avoir veu sur le pont Nostre-Dame de Paris trois ou quatre fort exquis, et qui sembleront merveilleux en ce pais pour la rareté de l'invention, entre lesquels celuy qui est faict en façon de poisson seroit, à mon opinion, le plus estymé, et si crois qu'il m'en cousteroit pas plus hault que deux ou trois cens escutz. Ces choses-là sont de peu de valeur et peuvent servir de beaucoup".

The gifts brought by the next ambassador, Jacques de Germigny, in 1579 were far more generous [3]. The Sultan received "un horloge sonnant les quarts d'heures et montrant tous les mouve-

---

[1] *Calendar of State Papers, Venice,* VIII, 1894, p. 85.
[2] Charrière, *l.c.,* III, 1853, 266 n. (letter dated May 8, 1572).
[3] The list of gifts has been published in 'Recueil des pieces choisies extraites sur les originaux de la Negotiation de Mr. de Germigny', printed as an appendix to *L'Illustre Orbândale ou l'histoire ancienne et moderne de la ville et cité de Chalon sur Saône,* 1622 (the pages are not numbered).

mens du Ciel, avec un Reveil", Mehmet the Grand Vizier "un grand horloge fait en tour garny de deux bouëttes de crystal de roche, avec le reveil et sonnant les heures seulement, ou estoient gravées les Armoires du Roy" [Henri III], the son of the Grand Vizier "un petit horologe sonnant, à prendre au col, garny d'or avec des rubis et emeraudes, ayant la bouëtte de crystal", and finally Rabbi Moses, the first physician of the Sultan, "un grand horloge".

4. Busbecq

Late in the year 1554 the Flemish humanist Ogier Ghiselin de Busbecq went to Turkey as Imperial ambassador. In the first of his famous Turkish Letters he tells that on the journey to Constantinople he experienced a "hardship almost worse than want of wine, and this was the dreadful way in which our nights were broken. Sometimes, in order to reach a good halting-place betimes, it was necessary to rise very early, while it was still dark. On these occasions it not infrequently happened that our Turkish guides mistook the moonlight for the approach of dawn, and proceeded to wake us soon after midnight in a most noisy fashion. For the Turks, you must know, have neither hours to mark their time, nor milestones to mark their roads. They have professional people called talismans [1], set apart for the service of their mosques (*templa*), who use a water-glass (*mensuris utuntur ex aqua*); and when these talismans know that morning is at hand, they utter a cry from a lofty minaret (*e celsa turri*) built for that special purpose, in order to call and invite the people to the performance of their devotions. They utter the same cry when one quarter of the day has elapsed, at midday, again when three quarters of the day are over, and, last of all, at sunset; each time

---

[1] "Talisman, en son sens actuel, n'apparaît qu'au XVIIe siècle; il se rattache, par l'arabe tilsim, au grec telesma. Mais talisman, du XIIIe au XVIIe siècle, a toujours désigné un 'prêtre musulman'. Ni Littré, ni Murray n'ont donné l'etymologie de ce premier mot, qui est une altération turque du persan dânichmand (savant), désignation des prêtres musulmans au moyen âge, bien connue, en particulier par des textes mongols et chinois" (P. Pelliot, *Revue archéologique*, 1932/I, 123).

repeating the cry in shrill quavering tones, the effect of which is not unpleasing, and the sound can be heard at a distance that would astonish you. Thus the Turks divide their day into four portions which are longer or shorter according to the season. They have no method for marking time during the night".

In order not to be disturbed in his sleep by false alarms, Busbecq told his Turkish guides that he had watches which could be trusted. "At first they would come early, and wake up my servant, bidding him go to me, and ask what the fingers of my timepieces said". Gradually they learned to rely on the watches of the stranger[1].

In his third letter, written in Constantinople in 1560, Busbecq came back to the subject[2]: "No nation in the world has shown greater readiness than the Turks to avail themselves of the useful inventions of foreigners, as is proved by their employment of cannons and mortars, and many other things invented by Christians. They cannot, however, be induced as yet to use printing, or to establish public clocks (*horologia in publico*), because they think that their scriptures—that is, their sacred books—would no longer be scriptures if they were printed, and that, if public clocks were introduced, the authority of their muezzins (*aeditui*) and their ancient rites would be thereby impaired".

In 1559, when some gifts from the Emperor arrived in Constantinople, it was Busbecq's duty to hand them over to the Sultan: "Süleyman desired me to present these gifts to him in the camp, in the sight of the army, as a fresh proof to his subjects that he and the Emperor were firm friends. He was anxious that such an idea should prevail, and also that an impression should be produced, that no warlike movement on the part of the Christians was likely to take place"[3]. These presents consisted of "some gilded cups and a clock of skilful workmanship, which

[1] C. T. Forster and F. H. B. Daniell, *The Life and Letters of O. G. de Busbecq*, 1881, I, 100-102. The original Latin text in A. G. Busbequius, *Omnia quae extant*, 1660, 20 f.

[2] Forster and Daniell, *l.c.*, I, 255; *Omnia quae extant*, 151.

[3] Forster and Daniell, *l.c.*, I, 297; *Omnia quae extant*, 174.

was mounted like a tower on the back of an elephant". This one is no longer in existence, but a number of clocks of this type exist and help us to visualize its appearance. One in the Kunsthistorisches Museum at Vienna (Fig. 7) is of particular interest in our context because the tower on the back of the elephant is crowned by the Turkish crescent, which seems to indicate that the clock was either intended as a gift for a Turk, or fulfilled this purpose and was later brought back to Austria [1]. The movement is contained in the howdah. The dial on the right shows the hours, that on the left is for the train which strikes the quarters. The eyes of the elephant are fixed to the balance, and therefore blink continually [2]. A second movement and wheels hidden in the ebony base propel the clock forwards on the table, while the mahout raises his arm, and the elephant moves its head and wags its tail.

Our clock, or rather automaton, is rather similar to that described and depicted in al-Jazarī's work (see above, pp. 8 f.). Was the Arabic treatise known in the West [3]? There is no evidence for it, and for the time being it is safer to say that the Renaissance clock-automata belong to the same tradition. Their driving power is, of course, different.

[1] Nothing seems to be known about its early history. Qu. von Leitner, *Die Schatzkammer*, 1882, 39, No. 68. *Katalog der Sammlung für Plastik und Kunstgewerbe*, Wien, II, No. 369 (as "Augsburg?, c. 1600"). Kl. Maurice, *Von Uhren und Automaten*, 1968, fig. 37.

[2] This trick has never failed to impress spectators. To connect the balance with the eyes of a figure is simple enough on a mechanical clock, but the idea is much older. We are told that on the late antique clock at Gaza every hour the Gorgo rolled her eyes in a terrifying way, and on the "Clock of Archimedes" there was a human face with eyes which hourly changed their colour (H. Diels, *Antike Technik*, 2. Aufl., 1920, 212, 221). On a clepsydra made for Khubilai Khan there were "dragons which opened their mouths and rolled their eyes as they chased the 'cloud pearls' which moved up and down" (Needham, *SCC*, IV/2, 505). Such figures of men, women and animals are common on mechanical clocks (see H. Alan Lloyd, *The Collector's Dictionary of Clocks*, 1964, s.v. Blinking Eye Clocks). What was once a toy worthy of an emperor became in the end an amusement for a rural population: Black Forest clocks from the seventies of the nineteenth century consist of the crouching figure of a turbaned Turk with the clock beneath his knees; his eyes blink, and at the stroke of the hour he opens his mouth (R. Mühe, *Die Historische Uhrensammlung Furtwangen*, 1967, fig. 43).

[3] This has been assumed by W. Born, 'Early European Automata', *The Connoisseur*, 100, 1937, 247, and R. Ettinghausen, 'Automata' (Islam), *Encyclopedia of World Art*, 2, 1960, 186.

5. The Austrian Tribute

By now every Turk in authority insisted on his share of clocks. Whenever the caravan of an ambassador approached the Turkish capital, their luggage resembled the shop of a clockmaker. On the way courtesy calls were paid on the local Pashas, clocks presented and their protection received. Once in Constantinople, a magnificent clock was given to the Grand Vizier and an even more costly one to the Sultan himself. More clocks were needed for the various influential court officials, all carefully graded according to their importance, and a little later it became customary to send extra clocks for the ladies in the Sultan's harem [1]. And spares had to be kept for the Pashas on the way back. But there were also occasions which could not be foreseen. It was dangerous for a Westerner to be seen with a watch in his pocket. Hans Dernschwam describes in his diary how the Austrian ambassador snatched his watch from him, as it was urgently needed for one of the viziers, to whom it was then given "in the name of king Ferdinand" [2].

The clocks which the Emperor sent every year to Constantinople are, if not always, fairly often described in contemporary documents. These descriptions can teach us something about clockmaking in the Late Renaissance. It would be completely wrong to assume that these clocks were of inferior workmanship, or outmoded, or that anything was deemed good enough for those "barbarians" beyond the frontier. Quite on the contrary, the leading clockmakers of the time were employed, those who

[1]   In 1590 Rudolph II sent to the Turkish *Kayserin* a small and a large *Uhr*, presumably a watch and a clock, the two together valued at 540 florins (A. H. Loebl, *Zur Geschichte der Türkenkriege von 1593-1606*, 1899, 117). In 1584 Catherine of Medici had sent various presents, among them a clock, to Nur Banu, the widow of Selim II and mother of Murad III. As Nur Banu had died in the meantime, it was decided to give the rest of the presents to the Sultana, but the clock to the Grand Vizier. Charrière, *l.c.*, IV, 1860, 275 n.: "Et avons trouvé plus expédient de présenter audict bassa l'horloge destiné pour ladicte sultane mère, comme de moindre estime et considération près ceux-cy pour etre façon d'Allemaigne et y avoir des figures". It was apparently an Augsburg automaton clock. It is of some interest to learn that the Sultana might have objected to the human figures on the clock.

[2]   H. Dernschwam, *Tagebuch einer Reise nach Konstantinopel und Kleinasien (1553/55)*, 1923, 32.

worked for the imperial court, like Hans Runggel, watchmaker in Augsburg (1566) [1], Gerhard Emmoser at Vienna, court clock-maker to Maximilian II (1568) [2], Hans Schlothaim at Augsburg (c. 1581) [3], Hans Paullus at Prague (1587) [4], or Georg Roll, of Augsburg (1589) [5]. Money was not spared to achieve perfection. Even for such a subordinate part as painting the case of a clock the leading painter at the court of Rudolph II, Bartholomeus Spranger, was employed [6].

The clocks became more and more ambitious, which meant that they were now the teamwork of clockmakers, goldsmiths, cabinet-makers, painters and specialists in mechanical music, a necessary division of labour which became even more complicated by the insistence of the various guilds that no outsider must ever perform a job which by law or tradition was their privilege. As a large number of craftsmen and artists had to work together and against time, it happened sometimes that the embassy could not

[1] For his biography see M. Bobinger, *Kunstuhrmacher in Alt-Augsburg*, 1969, 45 f., 61. *Jahrbuch der kunsthistorischen Sammlungen*, Vienna, 7, 1888, Reg. 5019 (payment for a clock which Maximilian II afterwards sent to Turkey).

[2] On September 5, 1568 he received payment for two watches (*uhrlein*) which Maximilian II had sent to Turkey (*Jahrbuch*, etc., 7, 1888, Reg. 5136). Emmoser came to Augsburg in 1563, but moved in 1566 to Vienna where he worked for the Emperors until his death in 1584. On him see A. Lhotsky, *Die Geschichte der Sammlungen* (Festschrift d. Kunsthist. Museums), I, 1941-45, pp. 173, 177, 273; E. Zinner, *Deutsche u. niederl. astron. Instrumente*, 2. Aufl., 1967, 303 f. His clock-driven celestial globe of 1579 is now in the Metropolitan Museum (A. von Bertele, *Globes and Spheres*, 1961, fig. 27; *Christina Queen of Sweden*, Exhibition Nationalmuseum Stockholm, 1966, No. 1225).

[3] See below, p. 37.

[4] Hans Paullus, *Glockenuhrmacher*, received money in 1587 for two clocks made for the Turkish embassy (*Jahrbuch*, etc., 7, 1888, Reg. 5473).

[5] On January 12, 1589 Roll received a sum of money in partial payment for a clock destined for the "Turkish present". On 24 June of the same year he was paid for an "uhrwerch oder globum celestem" (*Jahrbuch*, etc., 7, Reg. 5490). Bobinger assumed that the documents refer to the same order and that it might be identical with the celestial globe with clockwork now in the Osservatorio Astronomico at Naples which is signed "Georg Roll et Johannes Reinhold elaborabant Augustae 1589" (*l.c.*, 38, pl. 19). A final payment was made to Roll's widow in 1593 (*Jahrbuch*, 15, 1894, Reg. 11679). For a biography of Roll see Bobinger, *l.c.*, 29 ff. Roll seems to have been more a supplier and merchant than a clockmaker, and said himself that he bought clocks from other makers, altered them and signed them with his name.

[6] Payment in 1584 for "Abmalung einer Uhr zu der türkischen Verehrung" (E. Diez, *Jahrbuch*, etc., 28, 1909/10, 97). Or did he provide a sketch for such a clock? The word *Abmalung* can hardly have had this meaning.

leave for Turkey and was kept waiting in Vienna as the clocks had not yet arrived from Augsburg[1]. An even more embarrassing situation arose in 1606 when the clockmakers decided to keep back the gifts destined for the Sultan until the money due to them had been paid[2]. From time to time the Emperor had to deprive himself of some of his own clocks and watches and send them to Turkey[3]. Sometimes the clocks arrived only after the ambassadors had left. In such a case the Hapsburgs were glad to put such left-overs from the *Türkenverehrung* into their collections[4].

Türkenverehrung was the customary euphemism. After 1547, Austria had to pay a yearly tribute to Turkey, which consisted of a large sum of money, of silver vessels and of clocks[5]. It was understood that these silver vessels and clocks would always be of a new design[6]. Only the Turks spoke of a "tribute". The Austrians avoided the word as much as possible and preferred to

---

[1]   Baron Wenceslas Wratislaw, *Adventures ... Committed to Writing in the Year of Our Lord 1599*. Literally translated from the original Bohemian by A. H. Wratislaw, 1862, 1 f.: "We spent several months of that year [1592] at Vienna, waiting till the jewellery, watches, and other special presents, which our ambassador was to offer, not only to the Turkish emperor, but also to his pashas and grandees, were brought from Augsburg".

[2]   The Venetian ambassador reported this to the Doge with obvious glee (*Jahrbuch*, etc., 19, 1898, Reg. 16610).

[3]   We have already mentioned the clock by Hans Runggel (see p. 31). The planetarium sent by Ferdinand I is another case (above, p. 23).

[4]   Inventory of the possessions of Maximian II (1578), published *Jahrbuch*, etc., 13, 1892, p. XCI ff.: No. 490 (two watches "von der Türckhischen Verehrung uberblieben"), No. 623 (a cylindrical clock with glass case); the same happened with some silver vessels (*ibid.*, No. 176).

[5]   R. Lubenau, *Beschreibung der Reisen*, hrsg. von W. Sahm, I, 1914, 194: "Es haben die Kaiserliche Majestat Ferdinandus einen gewissen Frieden mit dem Turcken gemachet, welchen nachmahl Maximilianus und Rudolphus zu jeder Zeit verneuret, das kein Theil das ander auf der Grentzen bescheidigen oder einer dem anderen in sein Landt fallen sol. Davon dan ihre Kaiserliche Majestat dem Turcken ein jehrlich Praesent an Gelde, Silber und Uhrwergk senden mus. Danebenst einem oratorem nebenst etlichen vom Adel zu Constantinopel halten, welcher gleichsam als ein Geissel oder zum Pfande dahin gesandt, und nicht ehe von da gelassen wirdt, es komme den ein anderer, und wirdt jehrlich ein Nuncius mit der Praesent hineingesandt, welche Praesent von den Turcken ein Tribut oder Schatzung genandt wirdt".

[6]   Lubenau, *l.c.*, I, 200: "Das Present wirdt laudt den aufgerichten Pacten und Vertregen an Thalern, Silbergeschier und kostlichen Uhren gesandt, doch alle Jahr umgewechselt, das immer neue Ahrt von Uhren und Silbergeschirren gesandt werden".

call it a "present", a *Verehrung* [1]. The ambassadors had strict instructions that the bags with the tribute money should be handed over as discreetly as possible. The silver and the clocks were a different matter [2]. They were presented in a public ceremony, as their splendour would be interpreted as reflecting the wealth and the technical superiority of the donor.

There exist a few pictures of the audience ceremony where the clocks can be seen [3]. The illustration in the *Voyages en Turquie* of Lambert Wyts (1574) calls itself "Vray Pourtraict de La Salle de laudience du grand S[eigneu]r dedans son Pallais" (Fig. 8), but one's faith in the reliability of the picture is severely tested the moment one looks at the Flemish façade and courtyard with which the artist tried to "improve" the Saray. It may be unfair to single out these details, as otherwise the illustrations in the manuscript seem to be based on observation or at least on reliable drawings [4]. One of the gifts brought to the Sultan is a clock in a rock crystal case so that the movement becomes visible. Of later date is a gouache painting (Fig. 9) which shows the visit paid to the Pasha of Ofen by the Austrian ambassador Freiherr Johann Ludwig von Kuefstein (1628) [5]. The presents, consisting of a tall tower-shaped clock, two cups and a jug with basin, are carefully rendered.

The engraving after Johann Andreas Thelot (Fig. 10) is not a

[1] Lubenau, *l.c.*, I, 201: "Wier nennen es wol mit einem hoflichen Nahmen die Present. Aber der Turck nennet es Caratsch (*harac*), das ist Tribut".

[2] "Den 19.July [1587] nun in aller Frue hat man 45 000 Taller in sovil underschiedlichen Säcken auf 2 Kutschewägen geladen sambt einem grossen Uhrwerck, so da zum Tragen ungebreuchlich gewesen ... so ein meltes Geltt also gen Hoffe gelieffert, damit es unter den gemainen Man allhier nicht den Namen habe, das mir Iren Kayser soviel Geltt, so sie Tribut nennen, jerlich geben müssen. Den der gemain Man nachmals allein die Presentierung des Silbergeschmeidts sihet". (Jacob Führer von Haimendorf, *ap.* Lubenau, *l.c.*, II, 13).

[3] One such scene can be found in the "Manierenbuch" in the Library at Kassel (Ms. histor. 31, fol. 56); on this manuscript see E. Kunz, 'Reisebilder aus dem Orient', *Informationen* (*Kasseler Kulturkalender*), Jg. 4, No. 5, 1973, 10 f.

[4] Nationalbibliothek, Vienna, Ms. 3325*. *Bibliothèque Nationale d'Autriche. Manuscrits et livres imprimés concernant l'histoire des Pays-Bas*, Bruxelles 1962, No. 113.

[5] From a series of eleven gouache paintings with Turkish subjects in Schloss Greillenstein, Lower Austria. H. Tietze, *Die Denkmale des politischen Bezirkes Horn* (*Österr. Kunsttopographie*, 5), 1911, 482.

contemporary record, but a seventeenth-century reconstruction of the audience when the envoy of Rudolph II presented Murad III with a clock "in the shape of a castle, one might say a small seraglio ... At the stroke of the hour the gate opens and out comes the figure of the Sultan on horseback, followed by pashas, all of silver, and after having made their round the cavalcade disappears behind another gate. Then the bells announce the hours, and everything is so pleasant and magnificent that the Christians were amazed and the Turks enchanted" [1]. The gates which open and close by themselves, and the equestrian figures which appear and disappear to announce the hour, are familiar to us from a much older clock, the one sent by Harun ar-Rashid to Charlemagne [2].

Going through the documents describing the "presents for Turkey" one encounters a wide variety of shapes. Many of the clocks can be paralleled from existing examples in our collections but those sent to Turkey appear usually to be of a slightly earlier date. The clocks ordered by the Emperor as a gift for the Sultan often incorporated new ideas or inventions, which were afterwards turned out in numbers for the home market.

In general one can say that the clocks sent to Turkey were in no way different in character from those made for the Emperor and the mighty and wealthy of Christian Europe. The existence side by side of the didactic and the playful element, one might almost say of the astronomical observatory and the nursery, was in the spirit of the epoch. There was no condescension, nor any concession to a different taste. Only religious subjects were carefully avoided. The figures on the automata-clocks were usually put into Turkish dress, but even here one has to remember that exotic figures like Turks and Moors appear frequently

---

[1] *Die neu-eröffnete Ottomanische Pforte*, 1694, 288 (a German adaptation of the works by Sagredo and Rycaud). Sagredo gives the name of the Imperial envoy in a distorted form (Socmok for Sonnegk) and mixes up two successive embassies; his error has been rectified by J. von Hammer, *Geschichte des Osmanischen Reiches*, 2. verb. Aufl., 2, 1834, 536.

[2] See above, p. 7.

on clocks made for Western patrons. A clock in the shape of a turban was an exception and must have looked very odd[1]. Occasionally, one finds a detail introduced to please the recipient — as on the "magnificent fine clock with four towers in the Turkish fashion in the four corners, a clock which shows the time, strikes the hours and sounds the alarm"[2]. These towers "in the Turkish fashion" were presumably minaret-like structures crowned by crescents. This raises the question whether the finials with crescents one sees on some clocks in Late Renaissance style are an indication that these clocks were destined for Turkey. It seems very likely. The silver vessels which, together with the clocks, formed part of the tribute were sometimes of crescent shape[3]. Europeans knew that crescents decorated the top of minarets, and appeared on Turkish flags[4], and being heraldry-conscious they assumed that the crescent was the Turkish coat-of-arms long before this became a fact[5]. As we shall see, clocks made for export to Turkey in the eighteenth century show such finials with crescents.

Iconographic details of a purely Western character, like a figure of Death, are rare. In 1576 a Pasha received a striking clock on which hares, dogs and hunters appeared in succession,

---

[1] See below, p. 40.

[2] One of the gifts to the Sultan in the year 1575; the other two were a "writing-cabinet of gilt silver combined with a beautiful clock mounted in rock crystal", and a large compass with an engraved map of Turkey. All three objects were partly engraved, partly enamelled. S. Gerlach, *Tage-Buch*, 1674, 109 f.

[3] Or formed as a turban. The silver vessels are described in a list of 1592 (A. H. Loebl, *Zur Geschichte des Türkenkrieges von 1593-1606*, 1899, 119 ff., reprinted in O. Frass, *Quellenbuch zur österreichischen Geschichte*, 1959, II, 84 f.).

[4] "Und weill die thürne darzue gedient, dass man drauff vleissige Achtung auf solliche primam phasin Lunae gebe, daher vermuethet Scaliger, das Zeichen des Monds sei erstlich auff Thürne und also hernach in die Panir khommen ... Wol mag es auch sein, das solliche Feldzeichen seien ein gedächtnus des allergrössisten Wunderwerkhs, so dem Mahomed fälschlich zugemessen würt: nämlich wie er hab den halben Mond in sein Ermel verborgen". (J. Kepler, *Opera omnia*, ed. Ch. Frisch, 8/1, 1870, 303). That the crescents on minarets and banners were put there in memory of a miracle wrought by the Prophet was common belief in the West; cf. E. Cerulli, *Nuove ricerche sul Libro della Scala*, 1972, pp. 75 f., 239 f.

[5] A. Sakisian, 'Le croissant comme emblème national et religieux en Turquie', *Syria*, 22, 1941, 66-80. R. Ettinghausen, 'Hilal', *Encyclopaedia of Islam*, 2nd ed., 3, 1971, 384.

and finally a door opened and Death came out with an hour-glass in his hand [1]. Clocks where the mechanism set hunted and hunters into motion are known [2], and the figure of Death is, of course, frequently found on clocks, which in the Christian world were often regarded as a *memento mori*: "Unâ ex hisce morieris".

In the year 1576 on the same occasion as one Pasha received the clock with the figure of Death and the hunting scene, two of his colleagues had "globes which turn round once in twenty-four hours" [3]. These were probably not clock-driven mechanical globes, but a very popular type of spherical clock which rotated next to a standing human figure with an outstretched staff or sword, the tip of which indicated the hour. The short description of the clocks given away in 1576 does not mention any figures. If our identification is correct, it could have been any of the three existing versions of this clock [4]. On some the figure is a bearded man with a turban dressed in a short tunic [5], on others a blackamoor [6]. Provided our criterion of the finials with the crescent is correct, one such clock, now at Munich, was originally

[1]   Gerlach, *l.c.*, 279 f. ("laufen, wenn sie schlägt, nacheinander Hunde, Hasen und Jäger heraus. Item der Tod kommt zu einem Türlein heraus, hat ein Stundenglas in der Hand und so es ausgeschlagen, tut er die Tür wiederum zu").

[2]   On such a clock made in 1586 for Archduke Ferdinand II of Tyrol the clock-work even imitated the barking of the dogs (J. Hirn, *Erzherzog Ferdinand II. von Tirol*, 1888, II, 437 n. 4). A clock with a hunting scene dated "c. 1600" belongs to the Uhrenmuseum in Wuppertal (*Uhren im Wandel der Zeit. Eine Ausstellung im Deutschen Goldschmiedehaus Hanau*, 1964, fig. 33. J. Aberler, *5000 Jahre Zeitrechnung*, 1968, fig. 31).

[3]   Gerlach, *l.c.*, 279 f. ("Globen, die alle Tage einmal herumgehen").

[4]   The three types can be seen side by side in K. Maurice, *Von Uhren und Auto-maten*, 1968, figs. 57-59.

[5]   Bassermann-Jordan calls him an "astrologer", but the old inventories describe him as a "Turk" ("ein Schlag Uhr darauf ein Baum, auf welchem die Sphaera Coelestis, von einem Türcken haltendt", 1619 in the inventory of Archduke Maximilian I, *Archiv für die Kunde österr. Geschichts-Quellen*, 33, 1865, 292; 1626 inventory of Arch-duke Karl, *Jahrbuch der kunsthist. Sammlungen*, 33, 1916, p. V, No. 96, p. LXIV, No. 766). Examples exist in the Bayerisches Nationalmuseum, Munich (Maurice, *l.c.*, fig. 58), the Victoria and Albert Museum, London (636-1865), the Kunst-historisches Museum, Vienna (No. 395), the Pippa collection (L. Pippa, *Master-pieces of Watchmaking*, 1966, 76 f.), etc.

[6]   Examples are not rare, e.g. Kunsthistorisches Museum, Vienna (*Katalog d. Sammlung f. Plastik u. Kunstgewerbe*, II, 1966, Nos. 394, 397, 400), British Museum (88, 12-1, 119; E. Bruton, *Clocks and Watches*, 1968, 35). For others see Bassermann-Jordan, *Geschichte der Räderuhr*, 1905, 40 n.

made to be sent to Turkey; it belongs to a third type where the human figure is a savage scantily dressed in an apron of leaves [1].

The following year (1577) the Imperial ambassador gave away a clock in the hope that he would be able to liberate from prison a German nobleman. In the end the nobleman turned out to be an unfortunate stable-boy who had to pay dearly for his pretended identity. The clock which was wasted on that occasion was "beautiful and in the shape of a lion who, at the stroke of the hour, rolled his eyes and put out his tongue" [2]. Such lions were a speciality of the clockmakers of Augsburg in the Late Renaissance, and a number, showing the beast in a wide variety of postures [3], are still in existence.

A "Galleon" by Hans Schlothaim is easy to visualize [4], because he specialised in this type of table automaton, of which several survive [5]. The description of the one in the British Museum gives an excellent idea of these amazing toys [6]: "The ship was mounted on a wheeled carriage so that it could move along a table, propelled by its clockwork, which simultaneously caused its cannon in the bow to be fired. At the same time, a kidney-shaped disc fitted at the stern on the starboard side lifted a corner of the ship up

---

[1] Bayerisches Nationalmuseum, Munich. Bassermann-Jordan, *l.c.*, 22, 40, 79. Maurice, *l.c.*, fig. 59. E. Bassermann-Jordan and H. von Bertele, *The Book of Old Clocks and Watches*, 1964, fig. 127.

[2] Gerlach, *l.c.*, 354.

[3] One such lion who can do exactly the same tricks is in an English private collection: H. Alan Lloyd, *The Collector's Dictionary of Clocks*, 1964, 25 f., fig. 39 ("Augsburg, 16th century"). A clockmaker of the name of Philipp Trump produced a variant of the rotating sphere clock where the place of the Moor or Oriental has been taken by a lion rampant with blinking eyes and a protruding tongue (A. Chapuis and E. Gélis, *Le monde des automates*, 1928, I, 216 f.).

[4] Schlothaim had difficulties in finishing it punctually because "solche Arbeith schwer und kunstreich, die Zeit aber kurz" (the document has been printed by Chapuis & Gélis, *l.c.*, I, 196). In spring 1582 the *galera* had arrived at Prague, but had to be sent back to Augsburg for adjustments (*Jahrbuch, etc.* 15, 1894, Reg. 11956).

[5] Schlothaim had a forerunner in Caspar Wernher in Nuremberg, who had produced a similar ship (J. Neudörfer, *Nachrichten von Künstlern und Werkleuten*, hrsg. v. G. W. K. Lochner, 1875, 78).

[6] H. Tait, *Clocks in the British Museum*, 1968, 41. The galleon in the British Museum and a very similar one in the Musée de Cluny (now on loan to the Conservatoire des Arts et Métiers) in Paris show the figures of the seven Electors doing homage to the emperor. Schlothaim's authorship is attested by Philipp Hainhofer (O. Doering, *Hainhofer's Reisen*, 1901, 168 f.).

and then lowered it, simulating the rolling motion at sea. During this majestic progress, a fanfare would play on the small organ concealed below decks, activated by a pin-wheel and blown by automatic bellows. To the sound of this music ... the figures moved ... and even the drummers on the fo'c'sle gave a simulated roll on their drums and the trumpeters gave the impression of blowing their trumpets".

The "Galleon" given to the Sultan was in all likelihood similar and may also have possessed an organ. As we have seen, mechanical music and clocks have been intimately connected since Hellenistic times, but now at Augsburg, in these years, the old link between the two had become closer, thanks to new inventions [1]. The self-playing organ was a speciality of Augsburg. It started in Italy with the hydraulic works at Tivoli, but Georg Mayer brought the invention to Augsburg where it was taken up and improved upon by many of the clockmakers and organ-builders there [2]. In 1590 the Sultan received a "hohe Thurm-Uhr mit Singwerk" [3], presumably one of the automata with singing birds which in the Middle Ages had delighted Islamic and Byzantine rulers [4]. As we shall see, the new and at the same time very old invention was brought to perfection by Thomas Dallam [5].

Of the clocks sent to Turkey in 1592 we have a fairly detailed list which is interesting enough to be quoted here in its essentials [6].

[1]   On sixteenth-century clocks with mechanical music and puppets see A. Buchner, *Mechanical Musical Instruments*, 1959; A. Chapuis, *Histoire de la boîte à musique et de la musique mécanique*, 1955.

[2]   We are well informed about the early history of the self-playing organ at Augsburg thanks to a lawsuit about the priority of the invention. The documents have been found and published by E. F. Schmid, 'Hans Leo Hassler und seine Brüder. Neue Nachrichten zu ihrer Lebensgeschichte', *Zeitschrift des Historischen Vereins für Schwaben*, 54, 1941, 135 ff. See also Bobinger, *l.c.*, 49, on Erasmus Mayr, who pinned the cylinders for Schlothaim's musical automata.

[3]   Loebl, *l.c.*, 117.

[4]   G. Brett, 'The Automata in the Byzantine "Throne of Solomon" ', *Speculum*, 29, 1954, 477-487.

[5]   See below, p. 43.

[6]   There exist two slightly differing versions of the list. One is contained in the Memoirs of Baron Wenceslas Wratislaw, who took part in the embassy, *Adventures ... Committed to Writing in the Year of Our Lord 1599*, translated from the original Bohemian by A. H. Wratislaw, 1862. A somewhat shorter list in German was first published by Loebl, *l.c.*, 119 ff., and reprinted in Frass, *l.c.*, II, 84 f.

All the clocks had been manufactured at Augsburg[1]. The first five were destined for the Sultan:

(1) "A hexagonal ball, artistically adorned with chains, which twisted themselves surprisingly when the clock struck". It is as difficult to visualize this clock as to understand how it could have worked[2].

(2) "A clock in the shape of a tower, upon the striking of which Turkish jugglers in the different rooms ran about and peeped out".

(3) "A large square clock, a masterpiece of art, upon the striking whereof Turks ran out, mounted on horses and fought, and, when it left off striking, went in again".

(4) "A long clock, on which stood a wolf, carrying a goose in his mouth, on the striking of which the wolf fled, and a Turk hastened after him with his gun ready to shoot, and when the last stroke was about to strike, shot the wolf". The German list adds a further detail to the description of this extraordinary clock: the figure produced a sound like the howling of a wolf.

(5) "A large square smooth clock, on the top of which a Turk turned his eyes, and when it struck, moved his head and mouth". The German list reveals that the Turk could also waggle his ears.

(6) "A large clock in the form of a gilt horse, on which sat a Turk with an arrow drawn to the head".

(7) "A square striking-clock, on which two men stood and moved, and, when it struck, opened their mouths".

(8) "A hexagonal ball, like a *buzygan*, or Turkish mace, in which was a gilt striking-clock". Such a mace (*buzygan*, from Turkish *bosdoğan*) with a watch inside it exists in the Bayerisches National-museum, Munich (E. Bassermann-Jordan, *Die Geschichte der Räderuhr*, 1905, p. 74, pl. 8). An earlier example, perhaps the first one, is described in the codex of Benvenuto della Volpaia;

---

[1] Wratislaw, *l.c.*, 1 f.
[2] Wratislaw, *l.c.*, 64. The German list calls it a "silberne Kugel mit durch-brochener Kettenarbeit, die bei jedem Stundenschlag sich bewegte". This could be one of the falling ball clocks which descend on the chain from which they are suspended.

see A. Simoni, *Orologi italiani dal Cinquecento all'Ottocento*, 1965, 33 f., with a tentative reconstruction on pl. VII. It might seem odd to fix a watch into a deadly weapon the purpose of which was to crush the enemy's skull, but in case some horologically minded reader should be upset by such a rough treatment of a delicate watch, let him rest assured that by then, both in the East and in the West, the mace had become a staff of office or commander's baton.

(9) "A large clock in the shape of a sea-horse adorned all round with various shells" [1].

(10) "A clock like a Moor leading an English dog by a chain", The "English dog" (in German: *Dogge*) was in sixteenth-century Germany much esteemed for bull and bear-baiting. Such dogs appear often among the European presents to the Sultan; e.g. in 1563 Archduke Ferdinand sent an "English dog" and two striking-clocks to Turkey (*Vienna Jahrbuch*, XI, Reg. 7653). Once the English had established diplomatic relations with the Sublime Porte dogs were brought direct from England (see below, p. 42).

(11) "A clock, on which was a Turk sitting on horseback and behind him a lion overpowering another Turk, all which moved when the clock struck, and the horse pawed with his foot, and turned his eyes every minute". This clock would have appealed to Delacroix. It was an engraving by Antonio Tempesta which made Orientals on horseback hunting lions such a popular subject through the centuries.

(12) "A large gilt striking-clock, shaped like a Turkish turban upon which stood a chamois, which turned its eyes backwards and forwards and when the hour struck pawed with its foot and opened its mouth, and under this gilt serpents and scorpions twisted about". There are some zoological discrepancies between the two lists; in the German, Wratislaw's chamois appears as a horse, and his scorpions as lizards.

While none of these clocks seems to have survived, two clocks in the Kunsthistorisches Museum at Vienna deserve to be men-

---

[1]   Wratislaw, *l.c.*, 52 (also the following clocks).

tioned here, because they are so similar in construction and spirit that they would fit perfectly into our list. One (Fig. 11) is a boat with a box-like clock inside. Once the work has been wound up, the two oarsmen begin rowing, the standing Turkish captain raises his sabre, and the little monkey lifts his arms [1]. This clock may well have been made for the amusement of the Sultan, but nothing seems to be known about its early history. On the other hand, a clock with a Sultan on horseback has always been in the possession of the Hapsburgs and testifies to the widespread *turquerie* taste of the time (Fig. 12) [2]. The main figure is a Sultan who is accompanied by a soldier, a negro slave carrying a shield, and a dwarf with a monkey. The movements are the typical ones: the dog in front of the group jumps, the eyes of horse and rider roll, and the Sultan moves his arms. Similar figures exist elsewhere [3].

One has the impression that while in those years new ideas in clockmaking were constantly being tried out, watches remained more or less the same. The only innovation was that towards the end of the century metal cases went out of fashion and were replaced by cases of precious or semi-precious stones such as topaz and rock crystal [4].

[1]   Now at Castle Ambras (on loan from the Vienna Museum). Qu. von Leitner, *Die Schatzkammer*, 1882, p. 43, No. 79. W. Born, 'Early European Automata', *The Connoisseur*, 100, 1937, 250 f.

[2]   It is fully described in the inventory of 1619 (*Jahrbuch*, etc. 20, 1899, p. LXXXI, No. 1784), where the main figure is called a "Pasha", but the inventory of 1677 (*ibid.*, p. CXCII) speaks more convincingly of a "Turkish emperor"). Leitner, *l.c.*, p. 42, No. 77. *Katalog der Sammlung für Plastik und Kunstgewerbe*, Wien 1966, II, No. 399. Maurice, *l.c.*, fig. 54. A description of the Imperial Treasury in Vienna dating from 1659 singles out from the clocks "uno che rappresenta Maometto secondo Imperatore de' Turchi a cavallo. Il Turco è d'oro massiccio, il cavallo d'argento: e quando vuol battere le ore muove tutte due le gambe d'avanti a guisa di Corbetta, e manda fuori dalla bocca e dalle nari tanti nitriti, quanti esser dovriano li tocchi delle ore, fu donato dal Turco a Mattia Imperatore". (G. Campori, *Lettere artistiche inedite*, 1866, 113). This is presumably our clock with a few fanciful details added.

[3]   One at Dresden was described in 1629 as "a clock in the shape of a Turkish sultan, who moves his mace, the dog jumps and the horse moves its eyes" (O. Doering, *Des Augsburger Patriciers Ph. Hainhofer Reisen*, 1901, 173). Photographic reproduction in A. Chapuis and E. Gélis, *Le monde des automates*, 1928, I, fig. 158. A clock shown at the Exhibition of Muhammadan Art at Munich in 1910 (No. 2047) belonged apparently to the same reduced type without the attendant figures. There is one in the Nathan Collection (S. Guye and H. Michel, *Time and Space*, 1971, pl. II).

[4]   Loebl, *l.c.*, 117 (list of the presents sent to the Sultan by Rudolph II in 1590).

In 1606 with the peace treaty of Zsitvatorok the yearly tribute came to an end.

6. ENGLAND

The age of Queen Elizabeth was the period of great expansion for English trade. The English were out to conquer the Turkish market, and at the same time to gain the Sultan as a potential ally in a conflict with Spain. The ambassadors were the official representatives of the Queen, but their salaries were paid by the Turkey (later Levant) Company.

The first English ambassador to Turkey was William Harborne who, in 1583, was received in audience and presented the Sultan with precious textiles, silver vessels, a number of dogs of various breeds, and "one clocke, valued at five hundred pounds sterling: over it was a forest with trees of silver, among the which were deere chased with dogs, and men on horsebacke following, men drawing of water, others carrying mine oare on barrows: on the toppe of the clocke stood a castle, and on the castle a mill. All these were of silver. And the clocke was round beset with jewels" [1]. The clock was evidently similar to the one which the Emperor had presented in 1576 (see above, p. 35), but was infinitely richer.

A suitable gift had to be sent to Sultan Mehmet III after he had ascended the throne (1595). It was accepted from the first that the present could only be a clock. Sir Edward Barton, the English *chargé d'affaires* in Constantinople, suggested that Queen Elizabeth should send as her gift "a clock in form of a cock which I hear Her Highness hath in one of her palaces", which clock "may be somwhat beseeming to the bountifulness of so mighty a prince and worthy the person of so great an Emperor" [2]. But obviously

---

[1] R. Hakluyt, *The Principal Navigations*, 1904, V, 257. H. G. Rawlinson, 'The Embassy of William Harborne to Constantinople 1583-8', *Transactions of the Royal Historical Society*, 4th series, 5, 1922, 7. The actual sum paid for the clock was £ 304.8.6 (Sir William Foster, *The Travels of John Sanderson in the Levant*, 1931, 277). It was admired by the Venetian ambassador (*Calendar of State Papers, Venice*, 8, 1894, p. 55, No. 131).

[2] H. G. Rosedale, *Queen Elizabeth and the Levant Company*, 1904, 48, 50.

something more spectacular was needed to impress the Sultan, who by now had in his palace what must have been the largest collection of automata clocks in existence. In the end the Turkey Company decided on something really new, a self-playing organ combined with a clock [1]. On September 18, 1599, the Venetian ambassador could report to the Doge and Senate that the English present consisted "of an organ cunningly designed, which serves as a clock and can play several airs" [2].

The man who constructed the organ was Thomas Dallam, an organ-builder by profession. The Turkey Company insisted on Dallam's accompanying the present to Constantinople, a very wise precaution as the self-playing organ arrived there in a rather battered state. But Dallam and his three helpers were quickly able to repair all the damage the organ had suffered on its long sea voyage. Dallam himself wrote that he went to Turkey with "my mate Harvie, who was the ingener, Mr. Rowland Buckett, the paynter, and Myghell Watson the joyner". While Dallam was in charge of the whole and had constructed the organ, Harvie was apparently responsible for the clockwork. It has been suggested that he is the same person as the clockmaker Robert Harvey who was made a freeman of Oxford in 1588 [3]. The necessity of bringing a painter along makes it clear that the case was richly decorated. The ornamental paintings on the still existing organ at Hatfield House are a later work (1611) by the same Rowland Buckett [4].

Dallam wrote a fascinating account of his trip, in which he described how the Sultan came to listen to his organ [5]: "First the clocke strouke 22; then the chime of 16 bels went of, and played a song of 4 partes. That beinge done two personagis which stood

---

[1] Its history has been told in a thorough and entertaining book by Stanley Mayes, *An Organ for the Sultan*, 1956. See also C. B. Drover, 'Thomas Dallam's Organ Clock', *Antiquarian Horology*, March 1956.

[2] *Calendar of State Papers, Venice*, 9, 1897, No. 814.

[3] C. F. C. Beeson, *Clockmaking in Oxfordshire 1400-1850*, 1962, 119 f. E. L. Edwardes, *Weight-driven Chamber Clocks*, 1965, 137.

[4] E. Croft-Murray, *Decorative Painting in England 1537-1837*, I, 1962, 32, 194 f., pl. 75.

[5] Printed in J. Th. Bent, *Early Voyages and Travels in the Levant*, 1893.

upon two corners of the seconde storie, houldinge two silver trumpets in there handes, did lift them to theire heades, and sounded a tantarra. Than the muzicke went of, and the organ played a song of 5 partes twyse over. In the tope of the organ, being 16 foute hie, did stand a holly bush full of blacke birds and thrushis, which at the end of the musick did singe and shake their wynges. Divers other motions there was which the Grand Sinyor wondered at".

The Sultan was highly pleased. He might have been less pleased had he known that in the Middle Ages the Islamic countries had been leading in the construction of organs and musical automata.

7. THE FATE OF THE CLOCKS

What happened to all these marvels of human ingenuity? Today we find in the Topkapi Saray a remarkable collection of clocks and watches, but not a single one dates from the Renaissance period. Their ambitiousness, their incredibly complicated mechanisms which would have needed constant attention by a team of specialists, must have contributed to their early neglect and ultimate destruction.

The German Salomon Schweigger, not an unbiased observer who spent the years from 1578 to 1581 in the East, put the blame on the Turks. The beautiful silver vessels, which form part of the tribute, are at first admired, but soon go into the melting pot. The Sultan's fine clocks were piling up in one of the rooms of the palace. Those which had been brought some years before were already spoiled by rust. Some had been sold. Still, from time to time the Sultan has one brought to his apartments, and after a while exchanged for another [1].

One has a more favourable picture from a contemporary of Schweigger, Dominico Yerushalmi, a Jew who was for some time court physician to Murad III and later emigrated to Italy, where he was baptised in 1593. According to him there were pages

---

[1] S. Schweigger, *Ein newe Reyssbeschreibung*, 1608 (reprint 1964), 61 f.

in the palace who had been specially schooled to repair the clocks whenever this became necessary [1].

As we have seen, a number of Renaissance clocks in our collections seem to have been made expressly for Turkey, but one cannot be certain whether they did not reach their destination or were brought back at a later date. Presumably both these things happened [2].

Perhaps we should not rashly condemn the Turks for their neglect of their clocks. Of the many clock collections of the Renaissance hardly more than three (Vienna, Kassel, Dresden) have survived, at least in part, to our times. Of the collections of the Spanish Hapsburgs, the kings of France and England, the Medici, and so many others, practically nothing has come down to us except descriptions in old inventories.

8. THE PROVINCES

While clocks and watches were a common sight in the Turkish capital, the situation was entirely different in the provinces. A few clocks seem to have reached even the remotest corners of the Turkish Empire, but once they stopped ticking, who could put them right again?

The memoirs of Hans Ulrich Krafft give a vivid picture of life in a provincial town [3]. The unfortunate man spent the years from 1573 to 1577 in the Near East, much of it as a prisoner in Tripoli (Syria). A Turkish captain there had received from his brother in Hungary "two striking clocks made in Germany". One was a weight-driven wall-clock, the other a table-clock in a case of gilt

---

[1] His description of the Saray has been discovered and studied by E. Jacobs, 'Untersuchungen zur Geschichte der Bibliothek im Serai zu Konstantinopel', *Sitzungsberichte d. Heidelberger Akademie d. Wiss.*, 1919, pp. 64, 97n., and the synoptic table (column D, lines 60-66). Dominico's description exists in two recensions; the longer one contains an additional paragraph about sand clocks (*horologgi da polvere*) in the Saray, which are so large that they run the whole day without needing constant turning over. Provided the information is correct, these can not be sand-glasses, but must be clepsydras using sand instead of water.

[2] See above, p. 32.

[3] Hans Ulrich Krafft, *Reisen und Gefangenschaft*, hrsg. von K. D. Haszler, 1861, 195 ff., 247 ff.; a translation into modern German was published as *Denkwürdigkeiten*, hrsg. von A. Cohn, 1862, 251 ff., 311 ff., 339.

brass, and both needed attention. Krafft had no previous experience in clockmending, but he discovered what prevented the first from striking, and repaired it successfully. Here it was again, the clock with the head of a Hungarian carved in wood; whenever the clock struck, the head opened its mouth "exactly as the town clock on the market in Ulm"[1]. Krafft earned no gratitude. The owner was horrified by what he thought was a ghost; if Krafft would not remove the head at once, he would smash it to pieces with a hammer. Krafft had more luck with the table-clock. He earned a reputation as a skilful repairer and his condition in the prison improved. Even the Cadi came along with a clock. Krafft noticed that the spring of the striking-train was broken. The difficulty was to persuade a reluctant Greek goldsmith to rivet the broken spring; the Greek was afraid he might not succeed, and to incur the displeasure of a local tyrant was a serious matter.

At the court of the Sultan and in the houses of the Pashas there was no objection to human figures. Clockmakers in the West had not taken into consideration provincial bigotry, but here an easy remedy was at hand. "They like the small striking clocks which are brought from Germany; but if they show engraved figures, the Turks have them removed and replaced by flowers"[2].

The further away from the centre, the less use was a mechanical clock. One can understand the Georgian prince Qvarqvare who returned a beautiful clock given to him and asked instead for its value in cash; nobody at home would be able to handle it[3]. This was in Western Georgia, then a Turkish province. The situation was no better in Eastern Georgia which was a Persian sphere of influence. In 1598/99 Abel Pinçon met at Isfahan, at the court of Shah Abbas I, "an old Frenchman, a clock-maker, who is among

---

[1]   The clock which Hans Ulrich Krafft repaired was probably similar to a German seventeenth-century iron clock with the head of a man who moves his lower jaw when the hour strikes (illustrated in the sale catalogue Auktionshaus am Neumarkt W. Germann, Zürich, 12 June 1974, No. 107). On old public clocks with such "yawning" heads see E. v. Freydorf, *Zeitschrift für Kulturgeschichte*, 8, 1901, p. 391.

[3]   Samuel Kiechel (travelled in the East 1585-89), *Die Reisen*, hrsg. von K. D. Haszler, 1866, 266.

[2]   Schweigger, *l.c.*, 83.

the King's artisans; although he is decrepit and cannot work any longer the King keeps him by charity"[1]. The old man narrated his sad life-story. Originally "he had been quite comfortable in Constantinople, where he had plied his trade. He had, however, been induced by the words of Simon Khan, Prince of the Georgians, to leave Constantinople and to come to his country, where he promised him mountains and wonders. And, having charmed him by his tales, he took him to Zagan(?)[2] where, on arrival, he took from him all that he had in money and goods, made him his slave, and forced him by beating to work at his art down to the time of his extreme old age, and treated him as if he had bought him in a market". Only after ten years did he manage to flee to Persia. Pinçon told the adventures of the old clockmaker in order to contrast "the barbarity of a Christian prince and the kindness and humanity of a Muhammadan".

9. CLOCK-MAKERS IN SIXTEENTH-CENTURY TURKEY

We have seen that the foreign ambassadors arrived in Turkey with a clockmaker in their retinue. These men must have been very competent as their job was to see that the clocks handed over to the Sultan were in perfect condition at the presentation ceremony. They would have looked after the clocks in the legation, and presumably would not have refused an odd job here and there, but after a while they returned home with the ambassador. In a very few cases their names have come down[3]. They would not have been able to produce clocks of the type to which the Sultan and the dignitaries of the Turkish Empire were accustomed, as these had become team-work in which a dozen or more specialist craftsmen were involved.

---

[1] Pinçon's relation has been translated by Sir E. Denison Ross, *Sir Anthony Sherley and his Persian Adventure*, 1933, 158 f.

[2] "Zagan" is not more than a guess. The text says "Iapon", which is impossible (see also the review by P. Pelliot, *T'oung Pao*, 31, 1935, 169). Only an expert in Georgian history could tell us where Simon Khan resided at the time.

[3] 1577 Georg Klug (Gerlach, *l.c.*, 427; Schweigger, *l.c.*, 6); 1592 Blasius Cyrenthaller, "goldsmith and watchmaker" (Wratislaw, *l.c.*, 65). 1599 Dallam and Harvie (see above, p. 43).

There must have been many clockmakers, but chroniclers, both Western and Eastern, never regarded clocks or clockmakers as worthy of their attention. Even the invention of the mechanical clock had remained unnoticed. There were so many more interesting subjects to report—battles, court intrigues and diplomatic incidents. It is from just such a diplomatic incident that we learn with surprise that Sultan Süleyman had a French clockmaker in his employ, "maistre Guillaume l'orloger, qui racoustroit les orloges dudict Grand Turq et estoit sallarié de luy". When in 1547 the two French envoys quarrelled about who was the official ambassador of the Most Christian King, the Sultan decided to send his French-speaking clockmaker on a diplomatic mission to France, but the unfortunate man died on the way in Venice [1]. Murad III employed a clockmaker from Graz who was a prisoner of war; he was one of the hundred and fifty men who were needed to carry the dishes to the Sultan's table, but one assumes that his professional skill would have been available when needed [2].

The famous Grand Vizier Mehmet Pasha Sokullu (1505-1579) employed a renegade, a certain Oswald, as "clockmaker and steward". Oswald appears constantly in the Diary of Stephan Gerlach, but never in connection with clocks; the man was an inexhaustible source of local information and gossip [3]. A few more renegades and adventurers are mentioned, even an extremely versatile "Moor", presumably a North African, who began his career as a clockmaker, then became a schoolmaster and finally chief physician to the Sultan [4]. Whether any of them ever did more than repair-work is doubtful, but even that was of primary importance as the imported clocks and watches were useless if there was nobody who could look after them [5]. Outside

---

[1] J. Chesneau, *Le voyage de Monsieur d'Aramon*, publ. par Ch. Scheffer, 1887, pp. XXIX f., 19, 216.

[2] Gerlach, *l.c.*, 86 f.

[3] "Des Mehemet Bassan Uhrmacher und Truchsess"; Gerlach, *l.c.*, 238, 283, etc.

[4] Gerlach, *l.c.*, 87.

[5] A guild of clockmakers seems to have existed in Istanbul in 1582 (J. Hammer-Purgstall, *Geschichte des osman. Reiches*, IV, p. 627), but we do not know anything about its size or organisation, nor even whether these clockmakers produced mechanical clocks.

Constantinople even repair-work would not have been a full-time occupation. Augustin Marquart (ca. 1525-1566), a clock-maker from Augsburg, settled at Cairo, where he made a living as a clockmaker and gunsmith [1].

When the German traveller Reinhold Lubenau described Galata, the suburb of Constantinople (1587-89), he mentioned as living in a predominantly Turkish part of it "many German, English, French and Italian goldsmiths, clockmakers and gem-engravers, for the most part young people who return to Europe as soon as they have made some money" [2]. These birds of passage founded the colony of watchmakers in Galata which flourished in the seventeenth century.

10. TAQĪ AD-DĪN

High above these itinerant craftsmen stands Taqī ad-Dīn (Turkish: Takiyüddin; 1525-1585), a tragic figure, the lonely, frustrated innovator [3]. If we wish to learn something about the methods of clockmaking in the sixteenth century we have to turn to the East. The only technical treatise on the subject was written, not in Western Europe, but in Arabic by an Arab from Syria, Taqī ad-Dīn [4]. It dates from the late fifties of the sixteenth century. In the text the author mentions with some criticism a clock with the Lunar Mansions which he had seen in A.H. 966 (A.D. 1558), and in a note which he added to his finished work he

[1] Augustin Marquart made and repaired clocks for the local Pasha and his son, but he lived as an independent craftsman; see *Reyssbuch des heiligen Lands* (with a preface by S. Feyrabend), 1584, pp. 203v.ff. M. Bobinger, *Kunstuhrmacher in Alt-Augsburg*, 1969, 27, with reference to a paper which I have not seen: F. Lerner, 'Der Hofuhrmacher des Pascha in Kairo', *Die Uhr*, 1960, No. 7, p. 30.

[2] Lubenau, *l.c.*, I, 204; another reference to them (II, 16) shows that there were many Frenchmen among them.

[3] On him see J. H. Mordtmann, 'Das Observatorium des Taqī ed-din zu Pera', *Der Islam*, 13, 1923, 82-96, 282. A. Adnan, *La science chez les Turcs ottomans*, 1939, 77-80. A. Sayılı, 'Ala Al Dīn Al Manṣūr's Poem on the Istanbul Observatory', *Belleten*, 20, 1956, 429-484; the same, *The Observatory in Islam*, 1960, 289-305.

[4] S. Tekeli, *The Clocks in Ottoman Empire in 16th Century and Taqi al-Dīn's "The Brightest Stars for the Construction of the Mechanical Clocks"*, 1966, contains an edition of the text and translations into English and Turkish. E. Wiedemann and F. Hauser (*Über die Uhren im Bereich der islam. Kultur*, 1915, 10-16) had only translated the introductory chapters.

informs the reader that in A.H. 971 (A.D. 1563) he was ordered to construct a clock which indicated the times of Islamic prayer (and the months of the "Roman" calendar) [1]. Going through the pages of the treatise, which is now available in an English translation, one is reminded of al-Jazarī: the same clear, logical arrangement, and the same attention to practical details. Technical drawings in the text help to make the meaning clear. There is, however, an essential difference: the playful element which dominates al-Jazarī's work is entirely absent. He describes piece by piece how to construct the trains of his various clocks; in one single passage he refers to figures which move and make music and says that there exists an abundant literature on the subject to which he himself had contributed [2]. In the introduction he dismisses sand-glasses and waterclocks as old-fashioned and unreliable. He is only interested in the various types of weight-driven and spring-driven clocks.

Where did Taqī ad-Dīn acquire his knowledge? He himself says by studying the Western clocks in the house of his patron Pasha Ali [3]. Salomon Schweigger who lived in Constantinople at that time said, rightly or wrongly, that Taqī ad-Dīn had spent some years in Rome as a prisoner in the service of a mathematician.

His contemporaries paid no attention to his teaching. Disappointed, Taqī ad-Dīn turned to astronomy and astrology. Here again he was critical of the traditional methods. He built an astronomical observatory at Constantinople, for which he designed new instruments. These can be seen on a contemporary Turkish miniature which shows among them a spring-driven astronomical clock with several dials (Fig. 13a, b) [4].

The purpose of the observatory was to replace the unreliable and antiquated astronomical tables by new ones based on observa-

---

[1] Tekeli, *l.c.*, 91n., 183 f.
[2] Tekeli, *l.c.*, 183.
[3] On his identity see Wiedemann & Hauser, *l.c.*; Tekeli, *l.c.*, 140.
[4] On this "astronomical clock" see Adnan, *l.c.*, 78; Tekeli, *l.c.*, 130. F. Edhem and I. Stchoukine, *Les manuscrits orientaux illustrés de la Bibliothèque de l'Université de Stamboul*, 1933, pl. 3.

tion. The observatory had hardly started when it was razed to the ground. The Shayk al-Islam Qaḍīzāda told the Sultan that observing the stars would bring about disaster, and that no kingdom with an observatory had lasted for long. Murad III heeded his advice and ordered the immediate destruction of the observatory [1].

It is tempting to see Taqī ad-Dīn as the victim of religious fanaticism, as a typical case of science being strangled by obscurantism. But religious teaching had always included astronomy as indispensable for the determination of the correct times of prayer. Taqī ad-Dīn's position was hopeless; whether he wanted to teach men how to construct clocks or to correct the existing astronomical tables, his lonely struggle was doomed. The glorious tradition of Islamic science and technology was already dead by his time. It had been killed, not by the theologians, but by its own practitioners, the scholars and schoolmasters. Independent thinking, criticism, new research were no longer permitted. The old texts had been canonized, they were taught at school and had to be learned by rote. We have seen how Jazarī, in spite of all his admiration, did not shrink from criticising his Greek predecessors. Now Jazarī himself had become a classic, and the thirteenth-century book on water-clocks was still copied in the age of Galilei and Huyghens, in the same way as astronomy was taught from an elementary book written in the tenth century.

11. Georg Hartmann's Woodcut of a Sundial

Georg Hartmann of Nuremberg (1489-1564) is famous as a maker of scientific instruments. He also published a long series of woodcuts with designs of such instruments. Ernst Zinner, who studied and described his work, drew attention to one of these woodcuts, which is remarkable for its use of Arabic script and Islamic numerals (Fig. 14) [2]. A Latin inscription at the bottom of the sheet says: "Georgius Hartman Noremberge fatiebat

---

[1] It has been said that the Istanbul observatory influenced later European ones (*Encyclopaedia of Islam*, 2nd ed., 3, 1138). As it lasted only for a very short time, this seems most unlikely.

[2] E. Zinner, *Deutsche u. niederl. Instrumente*, 2. Aufl., 1956, pp. 95, 361, 363, 606.

Anno obsidionis". Professor Zinner took the words "anno obsidionis" to refer to the Turkish siege of Vienna in 1529, and concluded from it that the print was "certainly intended to be sold to the Turkish officers" [1]. But as Vienna is nowhere mentioned it seems obvious that "in the year of the siege" must refer to an event in the history of Nuremberg, and this can only be the siege of 1552, when the town came near to surrendering to Albert Achilles, Margrave of Brandenburg [2].

A transverse line divides the woodcut into fields which correspond to the vertical and the horizontal section of a diptych sundial. On top of the upper part appear Hartmann's first and second names and the word Nuremberg in Arabic script. Below it is an hour scale extending from 1 to 12. These would be *horae norimbergenses* which were counted *ab ortu solis* from one to twelve, and corresponded during daytime to the widely used "Babylonian hours". The line for ten o'clock has been left out, presumably by accident. The hours of the circle are marked 6 - 12 - 6. They are the *horae communes*, beginning at midnight, and correspond to our modern way of counting the hours. The crescent inside the circle seems to indicate that under certain conditions the sundial can also be used for telling the time from the shadow cast by the moon [3].

The lower part is the horizontal part of a folding sundial. In the centre is a compass, the needle of which is not due North-South, but shows a magnetic declination of East $10\frac{1}{2}°$ [4]. The margin of the compass serves as the third sundial; it is divided 5 - 12 - 7, which would suit places with a geographical latitude of under 45° [5]. The last hour scale gives the "Italian" *horae ab occasu solis*; as an indication of the night hours would be useless on a sundial, the numbering goes from 10 to 23.

---

[1] Zinner's interpretation has been accepted by Th. G. Werner, 'Nürnbergs Erzeugung und Ausfuhr wissenschaftlicher Geräte im Zeitalter der Entdeckungen', *Mitteilungen d. Vereins f. Geschichte d. Stadt Nürnberg*, 53, 1965, 114.

[2] On the events of this year see C. Headlam, *The Story of Nuremberg*, 1901, 86-89.

[3] Hartmann wrote a treatise on the use of the sundial as a moondial (Zinner, *l.c.*, 359).

[4] This is exactly the value given by Hartmann in one of his writings (Zinner, *l.c.*, 360).

[5] H.-G. Körber, *Zur Geschichte der Konstruktion von Sonnenuhren und Kompassen*, 1965, 111.

What was the purpose of this curious woodcut? Zinner thought it and the many similar ones by Hartmann were intended to be stuck on thin wooden boards [1]. In the seventeenth and eighteenth centuries this was a very common method of producing inexpensive scientific instruments, and that it was already known in the sixteenth century is evident from a number of woodcut gores for making globes [2]. However, in the case of Hartmann's woodcut the "Turkish officers" would have found the "do-it-yourself" equipment of little use. To fix a string as a gnomon to the two tablets would have been simple enough, but where could they find a compass of exactly the right size?

Hartmann himself gave the answer to this little problem. One of his woodcuts is inscribed "Pro utilitate horologistarum vulgo Compastmacher". Since the fifteenth century the manufacture of sundials with compasses had been a flourishing industry in Nuremberg, whose *Compastmacher* exported their products to many countries. They were, however, craftsmen and not mathematicians. Hartmann's little pieces of paper would provide them with the correct scales which could easily be traced on their ivory leaves. In the economic misery of the siege year it occurred to Hartmann that a new market could be opened up by producing sundials with Arabic lettering [3].

[1] Zinner, *l.c.*, 95.
[2] Zinner, *l.c.*, 363.
[3] In the very same year 1552 he designed a sundial plus compass for Jerusalem (Zinner, *l.c.*, 366).

CHAPTER II

THE SEVENTEENTH CENTURY

1. The Watchmakers of Galata

We now hear no longer about watchmakers attached to the embassies [1]. Their services were not needed, as a colony of watchmakers from Geneva had settled in Galata, the suburb and foreign quarter of Istanbul. We have seen how it had been established in the sixteenth century with the coming and going of young watchmakers, mainly French [2]. In the thirties of the seventeenth century a few men from Blois, a famous centre of watchmaking, had settled at Istanbul. Although coming from old families of watchmakers, they were merchants who ordered their goods not from their home town, but from Geneva. In 1632 one of them ordered from Anthoine Arlaud, "merchant watchmaker and burgher of Geneva", to be delivered in one year's time four round striking clocks with pierced silver cases, six oval lunar movement watches, and thirty plain oval watches. "The cases must be of silver, the dials and the plates supporting the movements are to be engraved, and the movements themselves are to be completely finished and gilt" [3].

Then a number of masters, Calvinists from Geneva, settled at Galata. It became an established practice that young men from Geneva, after having finished their apprenticeship, went to Turkey for three or four years to work there under one of their compatriots [4]. The process always began with an agreement

[1] One of the last was probably Abraham Ebert of Strassburg, who went with the Imperial embassy of 1616 (Adam Werner, *Ein gantz new Reysebuch*, 1622, 130).
[2] See above, p. 49.
[3] E. Develle, *Les horlogers blésois au XVIe et au XVIIe siècle*, 2 éd., 1917, 265, 378. E. Jaquet and A. Chapuis, *Technique and History of the Swiss Watch*, 1953, 23.
[4] A. Babel, 'Les métiers dans l'ancienne Genève. Histoire corporative de l'horlogerie, de l'orfèvrerie et des industries annexes', *Mémoires et documents publiés par la Société d'histoire et d'archéologie de Genève*, 33, 1916, 519-529. The same, 'L'horlogerie genevoise à Constantinople et dans le Levant du XVIe au XVIIIe siècle', *Étrennes genevoises*, 1927, 61-74.

drawn up at home, according to which the master undertook to pay the expenses of the voyage, in some cases even the ransom should his assistant happen to fall into the hands of pirates [1]. Undeterred by these very real dangers, the young men seem to have enjoyed the easy life in the East. Complaints about their way of life show that it did not always conform to Calvin's strict moral standards.

A watchmaker's shop in Galata in the seventeenth century would not have been different from a modern one in any part of the world: one would take one's clocks or watches there for repair, one could buy there, but only in rare cases would the goods have been made on the premises. The watchmakers and jewellers from Geneva were not the only ones to do business in Galata; others too, like the polyglot Jew Salomo who sold watches there, became aware that this was an ever-extending market [2]. The majority of the watches were evidently imported. It is of interest that one could order from Geneva *horloges à la turque* (1668, 1675) [3].

Others found it more profitable to sell watches made on the spot. In 1652 a watchmaker by the name of Barrachin undertook to go to Istanbul, where he would be paid ten *écus* for every *mouvement en blanc*, and twelve for every gilt one [4]. There were, of course, also watches put together on the spot, but from imported parts. The Swiss watch industry was by then already highly specialised, and watchmakers found it convenient to write home for springs and movements. In one year (1671) we hear of an order for sixty ordinary movements ready for gilding and forty movements *à lune* to be supplied by the watchmaker Jean-Anthoine Choudens [5].

A word should be said about these movements *à lune* which are constantly mentioned in the documents. We have already

[1] Babel, *Métiers, etc.*, 528, 569.
[2] C. J. Hiltebrandt, *Dreifache Schwedische Gesandtschaftsreise (1656-1658)*, hrsg. von F. Babinger, 1937, 132.
[3] Babel, *Métiers, etc.*, 526 n. 4; the same, *L'horlogerie, etc.*, 70.
[4] Babel, *L'horlogerie, etc.*, 68
[5] Jaquet and Chapuis, *l.c.*, 42.

seen how in 1632 a merchant from Blois ordered watches with a lunar movement from Geneva. The watch with lunar movement, or calendar or astronomical watch as it is also called, was the favourite form in the seventeenth century, both in the West and in the East. It is a miniature edition of the astronomical clocks of the sixteenth century [1]. A watch built to show not only the hour, but also the day, the weekday, the month, and the phases of the moon would need a profusion of dials, but their number could be drastically reduced by cutting volvelles, small apertures, into the dial or the plate which would show the relevant information, "5", "January", "Friday". Western watches often show tiny figures of the planet governing the day, e.g. Saturn for Saturday, but this is never found on watches made in or for Turkey, not only because figural subjects were carefully avoided, but also because the days of the week were not there called after the planets. There was, however, a conspicuous pictorial symbol which gave these watches their name, namely the disc of the moon which could be observed through the aperture in all its phases from invisible to full moon.

These lunar movement watches sold extremely well in Turkey. After all, they were in fashion everywhere, and they came in extremely handy in a world where both daily and religious life were based on the lunar calendar [2]. At the same time as the Swiss watch merchant at Galata ordered the forty lunar movements from Choudens, he placed an order with another Geneva watchmaker, Abraham Arlaud, for fifty watches of this particular type. That was in 1671. In 1676 the same Abraham Arlaud undertook to provide "as many lunar movement watches as he can make in the space of one year" [3].

The British Museum possesses a watch *à lune* made at Galata

---

[1]   Their method of construction was described by Taqī al-Dīn (Tekeli, *l.c.*, 174 ff.).

[2]   These Turkish calendar watches are mentioned among the masterpieces of watchmaking in the novel *Lotti, die Uhrmacherin* by Marie von Ebner-Eschenbach (1879; ch. III). In the heroine's collection were watches which "wussten Auskunft zu geben über die Sternzeit und nahmen Notiz vom türkischen Kalender".

[3]   Jaquet and Chapuis, *l.c.*, 29.

(Fig. 15a-b) [1]. The main dial is the lunar one with the 29 days of the month (plus a narrow gap for the 30th day), and inside the dial an aperture which shows the phases of the moon. Two more apertures to the left and right indicate the day of the week and the month. The hour dial (with divisions for the quarters and half-hours) has two concentric chapter-rings, the outer with Islamic, the inner with Roman numbers, the latter conceivably a replacement. The backplate is delicately engraved with a floral ornament. A silver cartouche fixed to it contains the Arabic signature: "The work of Dūnā [at] Galata".

The Arabic alphabet is not the ideal medium for rendering European names and we are left guessing what his real name might have been. Dunant would be one of several possiblities [2]. Whatever his name and nationality, it is evident that Dūnā set himself a very high standard in his watches, of which altogether three are at present known. The second of them has been in the Museum at Kassel since the eighteenth century (Fig. 16a-d) [3]. It is not a calendar watch and has only one dial, but one could not describe it as simple. The workmanship is superb, and even the key for winding up the watch is a work of art. The dial is inlaid with silver on a gilt ground, and real pearls are used both for the decoration (as on the pillars) and on the chapter-ring so that one can find the time in the dark by touch [4].

The third of the watches signed by him is now in the L. A. Mayer Memorial Museum in Jerusalem (Fig. 17) [5]. The chapter-ring with European numbers (concentric 1-12 and 13-24) is

---

[1] British Museum (88, 12-1, 174).

[2] The fatha in the second syllable is doubled as in an Arabic accusative in -an.

[3] First mentioned in an inventory of 1765, the watch came almost certainly from the Turkish war booty of 1717, when Hessian troops fought under Prince Eugène. I owe this information, the excellent photographs here reproduced and much help in studying the watch to the kindness of Dr. P. A. Kirchvogel. The watch has been mentioned by R. H. A. Miles, 'The Antiquarian Horological Society Tour', *Antiquarian Horology*, 5, 1965-68, 369.

[4] The pearls are a rare, but not unique feature; they occur on another watch made in Turkey in the seventeenth century (Christie's sale, February 16, 1971, No. 103; now at Jerusalem).

[5] Formerly in the S. N. Tonkin collection, New York (Sotheby's, November 13, 1967, No. 4).

evidently a later, but fairly early, replacement. Here too the decoration extends even to those parts not normally visible [1], as witness the engraved rinceaux on the spring barrel. The dial and the backplate are engraved on silver, the ornament being filled in with black and red sealing wax. The spiral rinceaux are remarkable both for their delicate execution and the fact that they are inspired by the ornament of Iznik pottery of the sixteenth century [2].

There exist a number of more or less similar watches, all made in or for Turkey in the seventeenth century. Signatures in Arabic script occur fairly frequently, but are usually more puzzling than helpful. The best known is a calendar watch in Vienna, booty from the battle of St. Gotthard, when the Imperial army defeated the Turks [3]. The dials still show the time when it stopped on the day of the battle, Friday, the 8 Muharram, i.e. the first of August, 1664. The watch is signed by two makers, whose names have been read as Waniek and Raabe [4].

The small watch shown in Fig. 18 is one of the rare cases where the signature can be read with ease: it is obviously a phonetic

---

[1] This is not quite correct. The watches of the time were hinged to the cases, which means that they could be viewed from all sides once one opened the outer case.

[2] E.g. A. Lane, *Later Islamic Pottery*, 1957, pl. 29A.

[3] Originally in the Schatzkammer, now in the Heeresmuseum. Qu. Leitner, *Die hervorragendsten Kunstwerke der Schatzkammer*, 1870-73, The same, *Die Schatzkammer des allerh. Kaiserhauses*, 1882, 14. G. Bilfinger, *Die mittelalterlichen Horen und die modernen Stunden*, 1892, 197. W. Erben, *Katalog des Heeresmuseums*, 4. Aufl., 1903, 119 f. *Ausstellung von Meisterwerken muhammedanischer Kunst*, Munich 1910, No. 1973. Georg Wagner, *Das Türkenjahr 1664*, 369. A. von Bertele, 'A Turkish Calendar Watch from the Middle of the Seventeenth Century', *Antiquarian Horology*, December 6, 1968, 12-14.

[4] There was a watchmaker Andreas Raeb in Hamburg, who in 1639 signed a calendar watch now in the Museum at Brussels (A.-M. Berryer and L. Dresse de Lebioles, *La mesure du temps*, 1961, pl. 10c). Its engraved decoration is, however, very different from the relief ornament of the watch in Vienna. For another of his calendar watches (one dated 1638) see L. Pippa, *Masterpieces of Watchmaking*, 1966, 82. Stylistic parallels to the Heeresmuseum watch are a watch of unknown ownership (ex Chester Beatty Collection; P. W. Cumhaill, *Investing in Clocks and Watches*, 1971, 67), and another in the Württembergisches Landesmuseum, Stuttgart (Inv. 1968/195), photographs of which I owe to the kindness of Dr. Volker Himmelein (G. H. Hostmann, *Taschenuhren früherer Jahrhunderte aus der Sammlung Marfels*, 1897, pl. 6. *Die Uhr, Zeitmesser und Schmuck, Ausstellung im Schmuckmuseum Pforzheim*, 1967, 110 f.).

spelling of Arlaud[1]. The Arlauds were a prolific family of watch-makers at Geneva, of whom we have already met two: Anthoine, whose works for Turkey are documented in 1632, and his son Abraham, who seems to have been particularly active in this field. Abraham had a nephew of the same name who in 1644, at the age of twenty, went to Istanbul[2]. Anthoine's dates are too early, which leaves us with the choice between the two Abrahams. The seemingly most trivial feature of this watch is perhaps its most remarkable one, namely the white enamel dial with the numbers in black. To us it seems the normal dial, but this particular fashion began only in the later seventeenth century[3]. The small size of the watch (47 mm.), but even more the unpretentious character of the painted decoration, a very modest wreath in red and blue, suggest that it was made in the East. Geneva was by then a famous centre of enamel painting, and a watch made there would have been more ambitious in its decoration[4].

Now we find for the first time side by side with the signatures of foreigners those of native watchmakers[5]. A calendar watch in the Saray (No. 16/1544) could easily be mistaken for the work of one of the Europeans in Galata, were it not for an inscription which proclaims it to be "the work of the famous Şeyh Dede 1114 (A.D. 1702)"[6].

Şahin, who signed a plate clock (diam. 20 cm.), now in the

[1] Formerly in the Tonkin collection, New York (sale Sotheby's, November 13, 1967, No. 10), now in the L. A. Mayer Memorial, Jerusalem. In the 18th or 19th century the watch was modernized by adding a balance and a curiously engraved cock.

[2] Jaquet and Chapuis (*l.c.* 29) do not distinguish between the two Abrahams. I follow here D. Gibertini, 'Liste des horlogers genevois du XVIe au milieu du XIXe siècle', *Genava*, n.s. 12, 1964, 218. Baillie (*Watchmakers*, 3rd ed., 1951, addenda p. XXV) says that Abraham (i.e. Abraham I) stayed in Istanbul 1647-51, 1666 and 1668. None of these authorities ever reveal the sources of their information.

[3] Berryer and Dresse de Lébioles, *l.c.*, 61 n. say: "Les cadrans en émail blanc apparaissent en France et en Suisse ver 1690 et en Angleterre dix années après". There exist isolated earlier examples.

[4] A "Turkish" watch by one of the Arlauds belongs to the Musée d'horlogerie at La Chaux-de-Fonds (No. 555; reproduced in the catalogue). It is impossible to say which member of the family made it.

[5] On these early Turkish watches see P. Ülkümen, 'Saatçiliğimiz', *Türk Etnografya Dergisi*, 4, 1961, 14-19.

[6] Ülkümen, *l.c.*, fig. 7.

Saray, decorated it in the Turkish taste. Covered with precious stones and with the numbers of the hours in white enamel on green ground, the clock is conceived in that exuberant style which is familiar to us from Turkish jewellery of the period, or from the gem-studded porcelain in the old collection of the Sultans [1]. But even here, or in a clock of similar shape by Bulugata [2], the inspiration came ultimately from the West, and particularly from the German plate clocks (*Telleruhren*) which were in fashion in the seventeenth century. These consist of a dial, an unusually broad rim, and a ring for suspension. Some of them are even heavily encrusted with semi-precious stones [3].

2. DIPLOMATIC GIFTS AND TRADE

The custom of sending clocks to the East as diplomatic gifts lived on in the seventeenth century. One appeared in audience with a clock under one's arm. A high standard was always maintained, though nobody ever asked whether the recipient would be able to appreciate the refinements of the workmanship. The clocks and watches by Thomas Tompion which William III sent to Algiers and to Tunis were certainly the best the leading clockmaker could produce in the golden age of English horology [4].

Although the yearly tribute had come to an end in the early seventeenth century, the Hapsburgs often had occasion to send costly presents to the Sultan. The tradition of ordering clocks and silverware from Augsburg continued. In 1655 an innovation was introduced: the dials of the forty-six clocks which the Emperor sent to Istanbul in that year were equipped "some with Turkish, and others with Christian figures" [5]. Gradually Europeans

---

[1]   C. E. Arseven, *Les arts decoratifs turcs*, 1952, fig. 383 f. *Splendeur de l'art turc*, Paris, Musée des arts décoratifs, 1953, No. 196, pl. 15. Ülkümen, *l.c.*, fig. 2-3. T. Öz, *The Topkapi Saray Museum, 50 Masterpieces*, n.d., pl. 31. A large reproduction in colour in *Türkiye. Revue publiée par la Direction Générale de la Presse*, No. 1, 1950, pl. 1.
[2]   *Splendeur de l'art turc*, etc., No. 195. Ülkümen, *l.c.*, fig. 4.
[3]   E. v. Bassermann-Jordan and H. v. Bertele, *The Book of Clocks and Watches*, 1964, p. 234, figs. 154-156.
[4]   R. W. Symonds, *Thomas Tompion, his Life and Work*, 1969, 124 f.
[5]   P. Rycaut, *The History of the Turkish Empire from the Year 1623 to the Year 1677*, 1680, part 2, p. 181 f.

learned that the figures used in the Islamic world looked different.

A few years ago such an Augsburg *Türkenuhr* turned up in the United States and was acquired for the Maximilianmuseum of its home town (Fig. 19). The clock, with its three dials, is signed by David Buschmann (1626-1701) [1]. Nothing is known about its early history except that, as is shown by its Islamic chapter-ring, it must have been made for Turkey. Here the natural exuber-ance of the late German Baroque ran riot as it was allied to the wish to appeal to an Eastern taste for colour, richness and precious stones. It has been stated that the jewels used for the decoration number almost 3,000, among them 2,020 garnets, 192 amethysts, 595 turquoises and 53 emeralds. The enamelled silver statuette on top looks like a Saint George, but he is wearing a kind of turban. Could he be a Turkish Saint George? In the seventeenth century Westerners learned with surprise and delight that their great warrior-saint was venerated among the infidels in the East [2]. To us, this does not seem particularly remarkable; we know that wherever people of different religions live side by side a certain syncretism arises, and that pilgrims flock to the sanctuaries of another faith when they hear of miracles and miraculous cures. But at the time this was exciting news, and might conceivably have brought about the choice of such a surprising subject [3].

Trade with the East seems to have been the monopoly of the watchmakers of Geneva, who provided both finished watches and single parts in considerable quantities. Otherwise there was very little direct trading. In the year 1607 a Frenchman bought on credit clocks and watches from Pierre Combret, clock maker at Lyon, and took them to Cairo and Alexandria. He returned to Lyon in 1610, apparently after a successful business trip [4]. No

---

[1] *Augsburger Barock, Ausstellung*, 1968, No. 577. M. Bobinger, *Kunstuhrmacher in Alt-Augsburg*, 1969, 93, 102. *Schriften des Fachkreises "Freude alter Uhren"*, Heft 10, 1970/71, 151.

[2] E. Jacobs, 'Untersuchungen zur Geschichte der Bibliothek im Serai', *Sitzungs-berichte der Heidelberger Akademie d. Wiss.*, 1919, pp. 33, 39, 47, 52.

[3] "Questo glorioso Santo è uno delli tre, che li Turchi communemente accettano per veri santi", wrote a contemporary (Jacobs, *l.c.*, 39 n.).

[4] E. Vial and C. Côte, *Les horlogers lyonnais de 1550 à 1650*, 1927, 19, 43, 238.

doubt there were other such enterprising merchants, but it seems unlikely that there were many of them. French seventeenth-century watches made for the East are rather uncommon[1].

Special interest attaches to the few English clocks made for Turkey, like the one by Edward Stanton (active 1662-1707)[2], as they foreshadow the flourishing export trade in the next century.

3. PERSIA AND INDIA

European clocks and watches had been arriving in Turkey for over a hundred years when the Persians began to show interest in them. In 1618, when the East India Company opened trade relations with Persia, their agents informed the authorities in London that the Shah wanted among other English goods "terrestrial and celestial globes of English make, beautiful pictures, a clock and watches, and looking glasses"[3].

Clocks and watches now appear constantly among the diplomatic gifts. Two adventurous clockmakers even went to Persia. This was very different from living under consular protection in the foreign quarter of Istanbul. The first of the two constructed under Shah Abbas (1587-1629) a much admired public clock in the market of Isfahan. He was an Englishman with the improbable name of Fesli; at least that is how his name has been transmitted. He killed a Persian, apparently in a brawl, and was himself killed in revenge by the family of his victim[4]. The second, Hans Rudolf Stadler, was Swiss. He had come to Istanbul with the Imperial legation in 1628, and from there he went to Persia where he produced a very small watch, just the size of an *écu*. Watches were then still a novelty in Persia; this one was given to Shah Safi I, who much admired it, wore it constantly, and took a

---

[1] Such a watch by Jean Hubert I is in the Metropolitan Museum (G. C. Williamson, *Stories of an Expert*, 1925, pl. 38; *Metropolitan Museum Bulletin*, January 1968, par. 62).

[2] P. G. Dawson, 'Clocks Made for the Turkish Market', *The Antique Collector*, 16, 1945, 96 f., fig. 1.

[3] *Calendar of State Papers, Colonial Series, East Indies 1617-21*, pp. 152, 159.

[4] A. Olearius, *Vermehrte Newe Beschreibung des Muscowitischen und Persischen Reyse*, 1656 (reprint 1971), 559.

liking to the clever watchmaker. But one night a man entered the house of Stadler, who shot him as a burglar. An infidel had killed a pious Muslim. Stadler was given the choice between death and conversion to Islam. He chose to die as a martyr for his faith [1].

This was the sad end of the two clockmakers and, at least for some time, of clockmaking in Persia. When in 1683 the famous traveller Jean Chardin talked to Evelyn about Persia he mentioned that the Persians "had neither clocks or watches", but he was wrong in thinking that the reason for their absence was the humidity of the air which made all iron rust [2].

In 1709 the Persians asked Louis XIV to send them "horlogeurs, graveurs et faiseurs d'instruments de mathématiques, architectes et habiles tailleurs de pierres et certains ingénieurs, inventeurs de machines et de nouveaux arts extraordinaires", but apparently nothing came of it [3].

It is odd to hear that the first watches to reach Mughal India should have come from Persia. In 1616 Shah Abbas sent to Jahangir an embassy with many gifts, among them "five clocks" [4]. Of course, the clocks were not of Persian workmanship, but it is impossible to state where they ultimately came from. They may have been brought from England to Persia, or possibly came via Turkey. Shah Abbas was in the habit of passing on some of the gifts he had himself received. In the previous year he had sent his "brother" Jahangir a share of the presents he had obtained from the Sultan of Turkey [5]. Thus the clocks could easily have come

[1] He was beheaded in 1637. His life story has been told, with considerable divergences in the details, by Olearius (*l.c.*, 520 f.) and by J. B. Tavernier, in whose company Stadler had travelled from Turkey to Persia (*Les six voyages*, 1676, I, 540-548).

[2] J. Evelyn, *The Diary*, ed. E. S. de Beer, 1955, vol. 4, 358. In 1679, Pierre-Didier Lagis (or Lagisse) died at Geneva, "ci-devant maistre orlogeur du Roy de Perse". Nothing else is known about his activities in Persia, but it is comforting to record that he at last returned safely to his native country (Babel, *Les métiers, etc.*, 529; the same, *L'horlogerie, etc.*, 73).

[3] *La Perse et la France, Relations diplomatiques et culturelles*, Exposition Musée Cernuschi, Paris 1972, No. 74.

[4] Sir William Foster, *The Embassy of Sir Thomas Roe to India*, 1926, 259.

[5] Abdur Rahim, 'Mughal Relations with Persia and Central Asia' (offprint from *Islamic Culture*, 8-9, 1934-35), 32.

from the Austrian tribute. Whatever their ultimate origin, we can be sure that they were superior to the clock which the first English ambassador Sir William Roe gave to Jahangir in 1616, and which the ambassador himself in his report mentioned as "a clock and two other trifles" [1].

At the same time an enterprising Englishman, Richard Steel, arrived in India with a painter and a smith who could make clocks. He reckoned on Jahangir buying their products, and on receiving the moiety [2]. As Steel returned home after some time, it seems that he failed in this as in other schemes.

Jahangir was evidently very proud of possessing what was not a timekeeper, but a clockwork automaton, a small group of Diana on a stag, which is conspicuously displayed on a miniature painted under his personal supervision and showing his own portrait together with that of the Shah of Persia [3]. The automaton is of German workmanship and dates from about 1600. Jahangir's contemporaries in Europe found the little group equally attractive, as is attested by the considerable number of versions still extant [4]. The Emperor Rudolph II sent one such group to the Grand Duke in Moscow [5], but kept what was apparently the original wax model in his own collection [6].

---

[1] Foster, *l.c.*, 94 n. 2.

[2] *Calendar of State Papers, Colonial Series, East Indies 1617-21*, 120. Foster, *l.c.*, 447.

[3] R. Ettinghausen, *Paintings of the Sultans and Emperors of India in American Collections*, 1961, pl. 13.

[4] They have been studied by G. Axel-Nilsson, Diana auf dem Hirsch, *Röhsska Konstslöjdmuseet Göteborg Arstryck*, 1950, 41-65, and addenda, *ibid.*, 1957, 55-58; K. A. Dietschy, 'Der Werthemannsche Hirsch und seine Verwandten', *Historisches Museum Basel, Jahresberichte*, 1967, 29-39.

[5] G. Tectander, *Iter persicum*, trad. Ch. Schefer, 1873, 73. Payment for the group was made in 1603 (*Jahrbuch der kunsthistorischen Sammlungen*, Vienna, 10, 1889, Reg. 5610).

[6] *Jahrbuch der kunsthistorischen Sammlungen*, Vienna, 25, 1905, p. XXX, No. 491.

CHAPTER III

THE EIGHTEENTH CENTURY

1. Sundials and Other Instruments

When discussing mediaeval Islamic astrolabes, we had occasion to notice that they were still appreciated and used by Western astronomers in the fifteenth century [1]. In the sixteenth century Islamic astrolabes were no longer regarded as of practical use, but they were still admired for their fine craftsmanship and thought worth keeping and collecting. King Philip II of Spain put into his art collection "two Arabic astrolabes and a planisphere" and two "Moresque astrolabes", all of which had belonged to Diego Hurtado de Mendoza (d. 1575), the famous statesman and man of letters [2]. We can only speculate on what were considered the distinctive features of "Arabic" and of "Moresque" astrolabes.

The new types of astrolabe evolved in sixteenth century Europe were in a few instances imitated in the East [3]. The seventeenth century saw the end of the astrolabe in Europe, where it had outlived its usefulness, and a new flowering of astrolabe construction in Persia and Mughal India, where very fine instruments were produced.

Many new types of instrument had been invented in the Renaissance, and Westerners were eager to find new markets for them. In 1600 the king of Morocco sent an embassy to England, the declared aim of which was to conclude an Anglo-Moroccan alliance for the purpose of attacking and then occupying Spain. The idea seemed so mad that the contemporaries thought that there must be something else behind it, and that the real aim of the

[1] See above, pp. 12, 14.
[2] F. J. Sánchez Cantón, *Inventarios reales. Bienes muebles que pertenecieron a Felipe II*, 1956-59, vol. 2, pp. 320, 323, 329.
[3] F. Maddison, 'Scientific Instruments', in *The Concise Encyclopaedia of Antiques*, ed. by L. G. G. Ramsey, 5, 1961, 196 n.; the same, 'Early Astronomical and Mathematical Instruments', *History of Science*, 2, 1963, 25.

5

unexpected visitors was trade espionage. What made them suspect was probably only a desire to familiarize themselves with—to them—a very strange country. The ship which carried them to England also brought a letter from Thomas Bernhere, an Englishman resident in "the citie of Maroco", to his brother-in-law, Edward Wright, a famous cosmographer and inventor of scientific instruments. The letter reads [1]:

"This King Muley Hamet is much delighted in the studie of Astronomy and Astrologie, and valueth Instruments serving for the course of the Sunne and Moone, that are of rare device, exceedingly. Wherefore your Spheare, your Watch, your Mundane Diall, and your Sextans, your new Magneticall Instrument for Declination, or any Astrolabe that hath somewhat extraordinarie in it will be accepted: and you might sell the same at good prices. Now with the Eagle there goe from hence certaine Ambassadors, and one of them is the Kings Secretarie, named Abdala Wahed Anoone, who has some insight in such matters. This Bearer my friend Master Pate, and Robert Kitchen the Master of the Ship, I thinke, will bring him unto you, unto whom I would have you shew all the varietie of Instruments that you have either in your owne hands, or have sold and lent to others; that hee may choose some for the Kings use and his owne. You may shew them also the Draughts and Lineaments of whatsoever you have in Paper, all of which I know will make them admire and be desirous to have some that they can understand how to use. You may cause to be framed some Instruments in Brasse or Silver, leaving the spaces for Arabique words and figures, and the words in Latine, or Spanish, which is farre better: there will be found here that can grave the same in Arabique upon the Instruments having some direction from you about the matter. Or Abdala Waked being a perfect Pen-man, can set the Arabique Letters, figures and words downe very faire; and so any of your Gravers can worke the same in Metall, having his Writing before them".

[1] S. Purchas, *Hakluytus Posthumus or Purchas his Pilgrims*, 1905, vol. 6, 57-59. B. Harris, 'A Portrait of a Moor', *Shakespeare Survey*, 11, 1958, 91. On Wright see E. G. R. Taylor, *The Mathematical Practitioners of Tudor and Stuart England*, 1967, 181 f.

Towards the end of his letter the writer adds: "Your Magneticall Instrument of Declination would be commodious for a yeerely Voyage, which some make for the King over a Sandy Sea (wherein they must use a Needle and Compasse) to Gago. If you question about the matter, and show them some instrument serving for this purpose, it will give great content".

When the agents of the English East India Company appeared in Persia for the first time, they made discreet enquiries what gifts would please the Shah. The list they received included "horizontal [sun-]dials which may answer to the latitude of Isfahan [1]". This demand seems surprising, as sundials had been produced in the East at all times and everywhere. But in the middle of the sixteenth century Georg Hartmann had already thought that the famous compass-dials made at Nuremberg would find a ready market in the Near East (see above, p. 51). The time was not yet ripe, as few people in the East possessed a watch.

Books on the history of time-measuring begin with the sundial and hurry on to the invention of mechanical clocks and watches. This is undoubtedly the correct historical sequence, but gives the completely wrong impression that with the arrival of the new invention sundials had become obsolete and lived on only as garden ornaments. Quite on the contrary, the more people possessed clocks and watches, the greater was the necessity to see whether these were fast or slow, and this became even more important with the improvements in time-keepers. To set them one had to find the correct time from a sundial. Thus we find in Europe a new industry coming into existence, the production of inexpensive, mass-produced, but reliable pocket sundials of pleasing exterior, which were also adjustable for different latitudes so that they could be used on a journey.

In the years around 1700 small sundials of metal became fashionable and were produced in great numbers, especially in France and England. One such dial, made by Edmund Culpeper

---

[1] *Calendar of State Papers, Colonial Series, East Indies 1617-21*, 159.

(1660-1738) in London, belonged once to a Moroccan, who had its underside engraved in Arabic script with the latitudes of Mecca and of three Moroccan towns (Tetuan, Meknes, and Marrakesh, in its old spelling as Maroko) [1]. Once you knew the latitude you could adjust the dial correspondingly, but as the owner left the hour-scale intact, one wonders how he puzzled out the meaning of its Roman numerals. The engraver used for the latitudes of the Islamic towns "Arabic" numerals, i.e. in the shape they had assumed in Europe. As anyone who has seen Moroccan coins knows, they had there a curious predilection for the European Arabic, as distinct from the Arabic Arabic, forms.

Of much greater interest are sundials expressly made for export. That reproduced here (Fig. 20 a, b) is made of silver and signed in Arabic "The work of Bion in Paris" [2]. Nicolas Bion (1652-1733) was in his time one of the leading makers of precision instruments, many of which are still in existence. This sundial is in every way identical with those which Bion made for the home market [3], except for the inclusion of a more Southern hour-scale (there are altogether four, for 35°, 40°, 45° and 50°) [4], and for the Arabic inscription, which are very competently engraved by someone who proudly signed his work *Mayir ḥakkāk*. The underside of the dial gives a list of place names with their latitudes in degrees and minutes. The right column lists Fez, Algiers, Tunis, Tripoli (in Lybia), Alexandria, Tripoli (in Lebanon), Cairo, Damietta and Jerusalem, the left Damascus, Aleppo, Cyprus, Crete, Iskenderon, Istanbul, Izmir, Thessaloniki, and, now we are outside the Islamic world, Venice. More cities within the Christian world are listed in the two concentric circles: in the

---

[1]   E. Weil, London, *Catalogue* 29, 1961, No. 196, 2 figs.

[2]   National Maritime Museum, Greenwich. Maddison, *Scientific Instruments,* etc., 193.

[3]   See, for example, one belonging to the Geomagnetisches Institut, Potsdam: H.-G. Körber, *Zur Geschichte der Konstruktion von Sonnenuhren*, 1965, p. 117, No. 13, pl. 24.

[4]   The scale for 35° could be used for any place between 32° and 37° as Bion himself points out in his textbook where he describes this type of sundial (*Traité de la construction et des principaux usages des instrumens de mathématique*, 3e éd., 1725, 367).

inner Madrid, Toulon, and Lisbon, and in the outer Naples, Vienna, Paris, Leghorn and Rome.

Sometimes Islamic makers of instruments took up more or less recent Western inventions like the nocturnal, an ingenious instrument designed to find the time at night [1]. It was invented in the early sixteenth century and remained in fashion for about two hundred years. One looks at the polar star through the hole in the centre, and adjusts the arm of the instrument to some stars near by, usually Alpha and Beta of the Great Bear. On a scale one can see, or even better feel by touch, the hour.

The armillary sphere became known, at least *in effigie*, in the year 1732 (Fig. 21), when the Hungarian renegade Ibrahim Müteferrika published in Istanbul his edition of the *Jihānnumā*. In the seventeenth century the famous scholar and bibliographer Kātib Çelebi (Ḥaji Halfa) had written a large geographical work, the *Jihānnumā*, the first attempt to combine the traditional geographical lore of the Islamic world with the learning of Western geographers [2]. Ibrahim Müteferrika, the man who brought book-printing to Turkey, brought this geographical work up-to-date and published it in 1732 [3]. The illustrations and maps were produced in a technique still new to the Islamic world, namely copper-engraving. The engraving with the armillary sphere is signed by Ahmed al-Qrimi.

Muhammadans must turn towards the shrine of the Kaʻba at Mecca when saying their prayers. To find the direction of Mecca needed complicated calculations, but soon after the Chinese invention of the magnetic compass needle became known in the Islamic world somebody had the idea of producing a compass

[1] An Islamic example, probably from the seventeenth century, in the History of Science Museum at Oxford, has been described by F. Maddison, *A Supplement to a Catalogue of Scientific Instruments in the Collection of J. A. Billmeir*, 1957, No. 238, pl. 32.

[2] F. Taeschner, 'Zur Geschichte des Djihānnumā', *Mitteilungen des Seminars für Orientalische Sprachen zu Berlin*, 29, Abt. 2, 1926, 99-111. A. Adnan, *La science chez les Turcs ottmans*, 1939, 103-120.

[3] Adnan, *l.c.*, 130-135. W. J. Watson, 'Ibrahim Müteferrika and Turkish Incunabula', *Journal of the American Oriental Society*, 88, 1968, 435-441.

specially designed for showing the *qibla*, the direction in which the prayers must be said [1]. One would think that such an intrinsically Islamic instrument as the *qibla* indicator would be immune to Western influences. Katib Çelebi, proud of his newly acquired Western knowledge, put certain questions to the Sheykh al-Islam, which he must have been sure would baffle the greatest authority in religious matters. Two of them were "How does one perform the five daily prayers and keep the Fast in places where there are six months of daylight and six months of night?", and "Is there any place other than Mecca where the *qibla* can be any of the four directions?" [2].

In the eighteenth century, a certain Baron was not worried about pious Muhammadans who would have to say their prayers among polar bears, but he assumed that they would have to perform their religious rites in many places of the Christian world. In 1151 H. (A.D. 1738) he produced a number of *qibla* indicators which are clearly inspired by Western sundials [3] (Fig. 22). They are real works of art, contained in round boxes painted with flowers in the Turkish "baroque" style, with a view of Mecca inside. The man who devised these indicators was an Armenian, Bedros Baronian or Baron, who served as interpreter first to the Dutch legation in Istanbul, and afterwards to that of the Kingdom of the Two Sicilies, and who translated a French geographical textbook into Turkish [4].

2. ROUSSEAU AND VOLTAIRE

Watchmaking in Turkey seems to have come to an end in the first years of the eighteenth century. The colony of watchmakers in Galata lingered on, but lost its importance. One of the last

---

[1]   Körber, *l.c.*, 98.

[2]   Katib Chelebi (Çelebi), *The Balance of Truth*, transl. by G. L. Lewis, 1957, 28.

[3]   Three of them are known to me: one in the Türk-Islam Eserleri Müzesi, Istanbul, the second in the Chester Beatty Library (V. Minorsky, *Catalogue of the Turkish Manuscripts*, 1958, No. 443; review by R. Ettinghausen, *Ars Orientalis*, 4, 1961, 392), and a third one which was given by the late Mrs. Vera Bryce Salomons to the L. A. Mayer Memorial in Jerusalem.

[4]   On Baron see Taeschner, *l.c.*, 109 f.; Adnan, *l.c.*, 136.

European watchmakers to go there was apparently Isaac Rousseau, whose main title to fame is that he was the father of Jean Jacques Rousseau. In his *Confessions* the son tells us [1]:

"My father, after the birth of my only brother, set off for Constantinople, where he had received the appointment of watchmaker to the Seraglio. During his absence, the beauty, wit, and accomplishments of my mother attracted a number of admirers, among whom M. de La Closure was the most assiduous in his attentions. His passion must have been extremely violent, since after a period of thirty years I have seen him deeply moved in speaking of her. My mother had a defence more powerful even than her virtue. She tenderly loved her husband. She pressed him to return. He gave up all his prospects, and hastened to Geneva. I was the unfortunate fruit of his return".

While Rousseau, although through no fault of his, had deprived the Turks of a watchmaker, his great adversary Voltaire helped to supply them with solid Swiss watches. Late in life Voltaire became the local squire at Ferney. His small community included some fifty religious refugees from Geneva who happened to be trained watchmakers. Voltaire set them to work in their new home, and used his boundless energy and numerous connections to open up new markets for them [2]. Turkey was the ideal place, because, as he wrote to Frederick the Great in 1771, "it is now sixty years since they have been importing watches from Geneva, and they are still not able to make one, or even to regulate it" [3]. Even the French ambassador in Turkey was pressed into the service of the philanthropic undertaking [4]. Voltaire hated the Turks as oppressors of the Greeks, but he had to admit that they were useful customers. A few years later, with the death of Voltaire in 1778, the enterprise came to a sudden end.

---

[1] Rousseau, *The Confessions*, newly transl. into English, 1891, 3.
[2] Voltaire, *Correspondence*, ed. Besterman; for the numerous references see the index s.v. Constantinople, Turkey and Watchmaking.
[3] *Correspondence*, 78, 127.
[4] *Ibid.*, 79, 131 f.

3. ENGLISH WATCHES FOR THE TURKISH MARKET

It is more than doubtful whether the watches which Voltaire had made at Ferney ever had any chance of conquering the Turkish market which by then was firmly in English hands. It was an export trade on a large scale. Visitors from the East went to the clockmaker's shop to make their purchases (Fig. 23)[1], but the bulk of the trade was shipped to Turkey by agents. Our information comes no longer from ambassadorial reports, but from trade documents. Writers of the time have often stressed the importance of this trade. Here are some references in chronological sequence:

1756. "Great quantities of watches are exported to Asia, particularly to Turkey; where they serve more for ornaments like pictures in rooms, than for use in the pockets" (R. Rolt, *A New Dictionary of Trade and Commerce*, s.v. Watch).

1761. "Clocks and watches now compose no inconsiderable branch of the commerce carried on by the Europeans to the East Indies and the Levant" (R. Rolt, *A New Dictionary*, etc., 2nd ed., s.v. Clock).

1778. [Among English goods sold in Turkey] "Watches, bracket and wall clocks. All clocks destined for the Turkish Empire have dials, not with Roman, but with Arabic chapters" (Fr. W. von Taube, *Abschilderung der Englischen Handlung*, 2. Aufl., 1778, vol. ii, p. 160).

1781. "England supplies metals, indigo and watches". (Quoted in H. Halm, *Habsburgischer Osthandel im 18. Jahrhundert*, 1954, p. 18).

1784. "The chief articles of their [the English] trade are lead, tin, watches, all sorts of clockwork..." (G. Habesci, *The Present State of the Ottoman Empire*, 1784, p. 428).

---

[1] Museum, Besançon. The picture has been called in turn Hogarth, French, English (?) about 1730, and North German. *Besançon, le plus ancien musée de France*, exhibition at the Musée des arts décoratifs, Paris 1957, p. 18, No. 41. Tardy, *La pendule française*, vol. 3, 352,

1797. "English watches, prepared for the Levant market, are more in demand than those of other Frank nations, and are one of the first articles of luxury that a Turk purchases or changes if he has money to spare" (J. Dallaway, *Constantinople Ancient and Modern*, 1797, p. 76).

By far the greatest demand was for watches, although clocks were by no means neglected. We shall have occasion to discuss two types which found particular favour, pendulum and musical clocks.

Clocks of a particularly luxurious type supposed to appeal to a very opulent Oriental taste are rather the exception. One, which reminds one of the clocks which were exported to China (see below, p. 90), was described in *The Gentleman's Magazine* for 1771 (p. 469): "Amongst the jewels of an eminent jeweller of this city, is a clock of exquisite workmanship, designed for the Grand Signor; the case is massy gold finely embossed, overlaid with diamonds, some as large as a guinea and larger, of the finest lustre; pearls as big as birds' eggs hang to two gold enameled trees that grow out of the gold rock, on which the clock stands, as its pedestal, a tree on each side the fruit of which is pearls, and leaves of emeralds, two great emeralds as big as pears are fixed on the two front pillars, the characters on the dial plate, which are Turkish, are of diamonds, as are the hands".

When on the subject of luxurious decoration one can hardly forbear to mention the most popular exhibit among the treasures of the Saray, one which thanks to the film *Topkapi* became internationally famous, the dagger with three enormous emeralds. Inside the hilt of this gem-studded and enamelled dagger one notices something far less spectacular—a small watch, made in London. As its dial of gold and enamel has Islamic chapters, it was specially made for Turkey. Thanks to Kemal Çığ the history of the dagger is now known: it was one of the gifts which Sultan Mahmud I sent to the Shah of Persia, Nadir Shah [1]. While the

---

[1] K. Çığ, *Topkapı Museum*, n.d., 52, with colour plate. A colour photograph which shows the dial of the watch can be seen in another guidebook: R. E. Koçu,

envoys were on their way, news reached them of the assassination of Nadir Shah (1747), and the intended gifts were taken back to Istanbul. A list of them has survived[1]; it contains several watches for the decoration of which a large number of diamonds, emeralds and rubies were used. It seems likely that these watches too were of English origin, but decorated and encrusted with jewels in Turkey[2].

Anybody who has ever looked at English eighteenth-century watches will be familiar with a very common type generally referred to as "with Turkish chapters" or "made for the Turkish market". "Turkish chapters" is, of course, nonsense. There are no Turkish numerals, only those which go with the Arabic script. Unfortunately, we cannot call them "Arabic", as we use that designation for our own numbers which are derived from the Islamic ones. "Watches for the Turkish market" is a much better designation, especially as the Turkish Empire then comprised Turkey proper and the Balkans, and, in fact or at least nominally, the larger part of the Arabic-speaking world.

The watches are easy to recognize. The dial gives the "Islamic" figures from 1-12, and the minutes from 5 to 60. At the back of the movement the regulator disc can be set from 1 to 6. The Turks liked many protecting cases. Usually there are two of silver, and a third either of tortoiseshell, or of shagreen leather (incidentally a method of tanning leather which is of Turkish origin). The owners of the watches sometimes added a locally made fourth case.

Most of these watches for the Turkish market are plain except for the balance cock which, as always in English eighteenth-century watches, is ornamented[3]. Where the outer case is deco-

---

A Guide to the Topkapı Palace Museum, 1966, 89. F. Preiger, 'The Imperial Treasury', *Apollo*, July 1970, 43.

[1]   Translated by J. von Hammer, *Histoire de l'empire ottoman*, vol. 15, 1839, 358 (the dagger), 360 (the watches).

[2]   In the collection of arms and armour in the Saray is a sword (labelled as "Persian") with enamel decoration in the same style as the dagger.

[3]   Watches with a "Turkish" dial but with mythological or other figural scenes do exist, but are rare, and in some instances one cannot even be sure whether watch and case really belong together.

rated, the intending purchaser had the choice between two types of still-life arrangement, one of special appeal to scholars, the other to military men. Still-life-type I is a nicely arranged group of scientific instruments, usually with a globe in the centre surrounded by a telescope, dividers, protractors and other emblems indicating the owner's learning. Of course, there is nothing specially Turkish about them; such groups were very common in European art [1].

While the scholarly instruments are only occasionally seen on watch cases, one can frequently find on them their military counterpart, a trophy, which seems to show that many army officers, but few scholars, could afford an expensive watch. The trophy is a picturesque grouping of arms and armour, cannons and mortars, with some flags in the background; it belongs to the tradition of classical art. Some craftsmen tried to flatter their Eastern customers by giving some local colour: they introduced a profusion of Turkish crescents or the horse-tail ensigns of a pasha. It was a back-handed compliment, as a tropaeum is a display of captured arms, but nobody seems to have minded, or even noticed it.

There were few eighteenth-century English watchmakers who did not occasionally produce a few watches for the Turkish market [2]. Here we have to restrict ourselves to those whose output was to a large extent, if not almost completely, destined for export.

One of them was Isaac Rogers (1754-1839) who exported thousands of watches to Turkey. For the benefit of his customers he took the trouble to sign them in Arabic script "The work of Ishaq Rogers". The letters are extremely clumsy, but it is quite

[1] An ornamental engraving by Pierre Ranson (1778) was intended to serve as a pattern for such groups (P. Jessen, *Meister des Ornamentstichs*, 1923, pl. 70).

[2] How did such small orders come about? Perhaps the answer was given by Josiah Bartholomew who in a different context, when complaining about some vexations by the customs authorities, mentioned incidentally: "I sometime since sold a dozen of silver watches of my own name to a person who was going to Turkey" (*British Parliamentary Papers. Reports of Committees*, 1817, Vol. VI, *Petitions of Watchmakers of Coventry*, p. 10).

wrong to speak of "bogus Turkish characters" [1]. The watch here reproduced (Fig. 24) shows on the inner case the hallmark for 1795, a year of feverish activity in which Rogers must have produced hundreds of such Turkish watches [2]. The backplate of the movement of an earlier watch exemplifies his Arabic signature (Fig. 25) [3]. When in 1817 a Parliamentary committee enquired into the depression in the watch industry, Isaac Rogers, "watch and clock manufacturer and merchant", was the principal witness. The answer he gave when asked about his activities provides an interesting glimpse of his export-import trade [4]: "What has been the nature of your operations in that trade?—The making of clocks and watches, and other mechanical works and manufactures, and exporting the same, and other merchandise to various parts of the world, receiving in return or as payment the products of those places".

While Isaac Rogers went in for a simple style, his contemporary Daniel de Saint Leu (London, 1753-1797) catered for wealthy Turkish customers who wanted their watches to be pieces of jewellery, preferably of gold, richly chased, and studded with diamonds. Two of his watches are still in the Saray, one with richly decorated hands, the other encrusted with diamonds [5]. One of his gold-and-diamond watches for the Eastern market shows a remarkable arrangement of musical instruments, all of a markedly

---

[1] A. Bird, *English House Clocks 1600-1850*, 1973, 140 (with a facsimile of such a signature).

[2] L. A. Mayer Memorial, Jerusalem. The serial number of the watch is 18,924. The numbering of the movements and silver cases of watches was demanded by law (25 George 3 cap. 64, sec. 4). On watches by I. Rogers with the hallmark for 1795 we find serial numbers ranging from 18,903 (Christie's, June 5, 1962, 73) to 19,542 (Christie's, October 7, 1969, 127).

[3] Metropolitan Museum of Art, New York (17.190.1426). Here reproduced from a photograph which I owe to my friend Richard Ettinghausen. "1759" is the serial number of the watch, not its date as stated by Williamson; Isaac Rogers was then five years old. G. C. Williamson, *Catalogue of the Collection of Watches the Property of J. Pierpont Morgan*, 1912, No. 198. Metropolitan Museum Bulletin, January 1968, 62.

[4] *British Parliamentary Papers, l.c.*, 39. On his commercial activities see also below, p. 78 n. 2.

[5] The Louvre possesses one of his works, the diamond-studded watch of the Dey of Algeria which the French captured at the conquest of Algiers in 1830 (J.-J. Marquet de Vasselot, *Catalogue sommaire de l'orfèvrerie*, 1914, No. 1020).

martial character [1]. One might describe them as partly Western, partly Oriental, were it not for the fact that even the Oriental ones now formed part of the outfit of every European military band, the kettle-drums since the end of the Middle Ages, the Jingling Johnnie, a staff with jingling bells, since the eighteenth century [2].

Ralph Gout (active 1770-1836) is another of the few English watchmakers who signed in Arabic script; he added "London" to his name. He had tried without success to export to Spain and to India. After his bankruptcy in 1796 he turned to the Turkish market, this time with evident success to judge by the large number of surviving Turkish watches with his name.

The names MARKWICK MARKHAM are frequently encountered on the dials of clocks and watches made for Turkey, either as these two names or as combined with a third one. The two names alone refer to the firm of Robert Markham who—it is said in 1730—succeeded his father-in-law James Markwick, and specialised in timepieces for Turkey which he produced in considerable quantities. Sometimes he had to call in outside help. In the British Museum can be seen a repeating watch inscribed on the dial "Markwick Markham London", while the movement is signed "W. Kipling 4734" [3]. This is apparently an instance of a watchmaker who, suddenly faced with an order so large that he could not fulfil it himself, had to buy movements from one of his colleagues.

Much more difficult to explain are the many watches and clocks which are signed "Markwick Markham" plus a third name. Was it somebody who continued the extinct firm under a modified name? Hardly, because even if we restrict ourselves to Turkish watches and clocks, no less than six different names appear combined with "Markwick Markham". They are Perigal, Peter Upjohn, H. Story, Borrell, John Johnson, and Recordon. Did these men

[1] Sale Sotheby's, May 2, 1966, 178.
[2] H. G. Farmer, 'Turkish Crescent, or Jingling Johnnie', in *Grove's Dictionary of Music and Musicians*, Vol. 8, 1954, 612 f.
[3] British Museum (CAI-648). William Kipling also supplied movements for George Prior (British Museum, CAI-650) and himself made complete watches for Turkey (*ibid.*, CAI-649).

simply want to cash in on the reputation the old firm had acquired in Turkey? Probably, but some of them sold their products there also under their own name. The fame the "Markwick Markham" watches enjoyed in Turkey is attested by old forgeries of continental origin [1].

For many years the Turkish market was dominated by George Prior, who like Isaac Rogers combined the export of English watches with the import of Near Eastern goods [2]. In his early years he was unable to cope with the flood of orders, and had to buy movements wholesale from his English fellow watchmakers, occasionally even from abroad [3]. By the end of his life he must have sent between forty and fifty thousand watches to Turkey [4]. To help collectors and museum officials in dating their watches I give here a few selected serial numbers and dates [5]:

> 6,053:   1772 (Christie's, 10 October 1961, lot 7)
> 15,888:   1784 (Sotheby's, 22 January 1973, lot 165)
> 21,686:   1793 (British Museum CAI-2378)
> 28,674:   1800 (L. Pippa, *Masterpieces of Watchmaking*, 1966, pp. 136 f.)
> 35,821:   1810 (Christie's, 10 October 1961, lot 4).

[1]   As an example one could quote a watch signed on the movements in faulty spelling MARKWICH MARKAM LONDON 8219 (Christie's, October 23, 1974, 165).

[2]   On March 31, 1790, both he and Isaac Rogers attended a meeting of the "Merchants concerned in the trade to Levant-Seas" "to consider of the most effectual measure for preventing the abuses which have prevailed latterly in the Conveyance of merchandize from different parts of Turkey to London" (Guildhall Library, London, Broadsides, 7.43. I owe this reference to the kind interest of Mr. I. F. Maxted).

[3]   Some of his watches contain signed movements by Benjamin Barber (who also on his own made clocks and watches for Turkey), William Morgan, William Kipling, and others. Worth mentioning is a watch by George Prior with a movement signed "Bened.o Hochenadl Venezia" (Sotheby's, July 12, 1971, 135; in the catalogue the signature is misprinted).

[4]   As George Prior put numbers on his own watch movements, but not on those he had bought from others, it is impossible to be sure of the total. The highest serial number known to me is 41,898, which dates from 1813 (Christie's, February 27, 1973, 155). No. 42,003, hallmarked 1816, shows the name of George Prior on the dial, but the movement is already the work of his son Edward.

[5]   Wherever hallmark and serial number do not agree, the watch ought to be examined carefully; e.g. a watch in the British Museum (CAI-542) is numbered 16,620, while the hinged silver case is hallmarked 1797. Mr B. Hutchinson pointed out to me that the dial shows signs of having been ground to fit the present case which is certainly not the original one.

In Turkey the name of George Prior on the dial was regarded as a guarantee of good workmanship, a fact which was exploited by dishonest Swiss firms which put inferior but cheap forgeries on the market, all with the fraudulent signature of George Prior [1]. Figure 26a-c shows one of these early forgeries [2]. The words "George Prior" are clumsily and hesitatingly written as if by a schoolchild, each word between two lines. The movement is French, with a bridge instead of a cock, and the outer case is decorated with foliage in relief and cheap paste jewellery. Nothing resembles George Prior's authentic watches; only his famous name has been used to make it more saleable.

We shall see how his son Edward continued the father's flourishing business. Although watches from other countries arrived in Turkey, from France, from Italy, even from Denmark, the English dominated the market.

4. Pendulum Clocks

Watches were not the only line English craftsmen had to offer; pendulum clocks too found a ready market in Turkey, although only at a slightly later date. With the invention of the pendulum clock in the seventeenth century precise time-keeping had at last become possible. While Europe was still discussing this amazing new invention and arguing whether the priority belonged to Galilei or to Huygens, somebody came forward with the surprising claim that the real inventors of the pendulum clock were the Arabs [3]. The extraordinary idea that mediaeval Arabic clocks could have been regulated by a pendulum was widely believed [4]. E. Wiedemann has shown how the misunderstanding came about: what looked like a pendulum in the illustrations of mediaeval Arabic manuscripts was in reality a plumb-line [5].

[1] Swiss forgeries of George Prior watches made by Georges Achard at Geneva in 1806 and sold at Smyrna are mentioned by A. Babel, *Les métiers, etc.* (see above, p. 54 n. 4), 519; the same, *L'horlogerie, etc.*, 73.

[2] British Museum (CAI-815).

[3] E. Bernard, 'The Longitudes ... of the Chiefest Fixt Stars', *Philosophical Transactions*, 14, No. 158, April 1684, 567.

[4] Among others by Alexander von Humboldt, *Kosmos*, 1847, 2, 258.

[5] E. Wiedemann, 'Über die angebliche Verwendung des Pendels zur Zeitmessung

Bringing pendulum clocks to Turkey was not as easy as it might appear. In the year 1680, not so long after the new invention had been made, the English ambassador to the Sublime Porte, Sir John Finch, thought of modernizing the traditional "gifts" by including among them a telescope and a "rare pendulum", but as the Grand Vizier expected a large sum of money, the gifts were refused [1]. In 1699 a new French ambassador arrived in Istanbul. He brought with him a magnificent *pendule* with a dial marked *à la turque* destined for the Grand Vizier, and an even more magnificent one for the Sultan. But when he was about to enter the audience chamber, the proud ambassador of Louis XIV refused to give up his sword. The audience never took place, and the presents were returned to the ambassador [2]. In spite of these initial setbacks pendulum clocks did eventually arrive in the Saray. When a new French ambassador arrived in Turkey in 1716, he successfully delivered at the Sublime Porte *une magnifique pendule* for the Grand Vizier and *deux magnifiques pendules* for the Sultan himself [3].

More and more such pendulum clocks arrived at the Palace and needed expert attention. Being heavy and bulky and not easily movable, it became necessary to allow an infidel, a Christian clockmaker from Galata, to enter from time to time the innermost and normally inaccessible rooms of the palace. A. de la Motraye, the French traveller, profited from these circumstances. He made friends with the clockmaker in charge of the palace clocks, who was a fellow Protestant, and disguised as his mate and carrying some tools he managed to see the forbidden parts of the Saray. The two clockmakers, the real and the pretended one, were

bei den Arabern', *Berichte der Deutschen Physikalischen Gesellschaft*, 1919, 663 f.; and addendum under the same title in *Zeitschrift für Physik*, 10, 1922, 267 f.

[1] G. F. Abbott, *Under the Turk in Constantinople. A Record of Sir John Finch's Embassy 1674-1681*, 1920, 318.

[2] J. Pitton de Tournefort, *Relation d'un voyage du Levant fait par ordre du roy*, I, 1717, 535. A. de la Motraye, *Travels through Europe, Asia and Part of Africa*, 1730, I, 200.

[3] Ch. Schefer, *Mémoire historique sur l'ambassade de France à Constantinople par le marquis de Bonnac*, 1894, p. XXXII f.

closely watched by an eunuch when they entered the harem, and, needless to say, the ladies were out of sight. Thus Motraye was not distracted when he admired the luxurious furnishings of their apartments and, of course, there were the clocks which needed attention. "The Eunuch conducted us into a Hall of the Harem, which seem'd to me finest and most agreeable of any in the Seraglio, where an English Clock, with a magnificent Case and Stand, wanted his Assistance to rectify it". There was much to be seen and described in this hall. "After the Clock in the Hall was put in Order, the Eunuch made us pass by several little Chambers with Doors shut, like the Cells of Monks or Nuns, as far as I cou'd judge by one that another Eunuch open'd, ... In this Chamber there was a very fine Pendulum to be mended, the Case of which was inlaid with Pieces of Mother of Pearl. Gold and Silver. It was upon a Massy Silver Table, after our Fashion, before a Looking Glass, the Frame of which was of Silver gilt, curiously work'd, and embellished with Foliages in Relievo... There was nothing to be done to the Pendulum, but to make it go faster, for it lost, as the Eunuch said, who had the Key of the Chamber, an Hour in Twenty four; nevertheless the Watch-maker was long enough about it, to give me time to observe what was in the Chamber. After which the Eunuchs reconducted us back again, and delivered us into the Care of two Hassekis (A sort of Messengers), who led us to the Door of a Room that looked upon the Garden, where there was another Clock so much out of Order, that the Watch-maker said he must carry it home to mend it, for which reason it was taken down. These Clocks, or Pendulums, this Table and Stands, with the Looking-Glass after the manner of the Franks, and several other Things that one meets up and down the Seraglio, that are fitted up to the Turkish Taste, are Presents that have been made by Ambassadors when they received Audience of the Grand Seignior [1]".

The obliging man in charge of the palace clocks who had

[1] A. de la Motraye, *l.c.*, I, 172 f.

taken Motraye inside the Saray told him also about an anxious moment when the very existence of the colony of Genevan watchmakers was threatened. They lived traditionally under the protection of the French ambassador, but were Calvinists. When after the revocation of the Edict of Nantes (1685) Pierre Girardin, the French ambassador (1686-89), had begun to repatriate all Huguenots, the Turks came to their rescue. The Grand Vizier claimed one of them as his personal watchmaker, and other Turkish dignitaries followed his example. Paris had to give in.

The majority of the imported pendulum clocks were of English manufacture. Even to-day one can see in the Saray opposite the entrance to the Circumcision Room an English long-case clock [1]. It is by no means the only English "grandfather clock" in Istanbul. In the great mosques of Istanbul there is so much to admire that few tourists will stop in front of the English long-case clocks which can be found everywhere. One by Edward Prior with a base decorated in intarsia with a trophy of swords and flags can be seen in Hagia Sophia. The Mosque of Sultan Ahmed I even has two, one again by the ubiquitous Edward Prior, the other, signed in English and Arabic, by Ralph Gout.

In the sixteenth century Busbecq had spoken of the Turkish resistance to the introduction of public clocks as they were incompatible with the institution of the muezzin. The call for prayer was never abolished, but now the muezzin ascended the minaret after having learned from the pendulum clock that it was the right time for his call. One would like to know how it came about that at a certain date, possibly only in the early nineteenth century, pendulum clocks became part of the necessary furnishings of a mosque or a dervish convent [2]. Once admitted into the mosques the fashion for pendulum clocks spread from them to the Greek Orthodox churches [3].

---

[1]   It is signed "Wm Jourdain London". On William Jourdain see a short note in *The Horological Journal*, 42, 1900, 132.

[2]   Th. Menzel, 'Das Bektaši-Kloster Sejjid-i-Ghâzi', *Mitteilungen des Seminars f. Orientalische Sprachen*, 28, 1925, 112.

[3]   An amusing example can be seen in the church of Hagios Antonios at Nicosia, Cyprus, a richly decorated long-case clock with a dial with Islamic numerals, and a rocking-ship automaton at the pendulum.

For many centuries Muhammadans had found the times of prayer by the traditional methods, mainly by using an astrolabe or a quadrant [1]. In fact the exact determination of the hours had become a branch of learning in its own right which could always justify its existence by the needs of the religious rites. The introduction of the mechanical clock into the mosque was a revolutionary step, but it was a silent revolution. There was no public outcry, no conservative resistance; there may even have been hidden relief that a much simpler method had now been found. Of course, one needed tables which showed the correlation between the hours "o'clock" and the prayer hours which changed with the times of the year, but this presented no particular difficulty. In theological colleges the old method of fixing the hours of prayer with the help of the quadrant was still taught at the beginning of our century, and probably still is, but it had become book learning [2].

Mechanical clocks work on the principle of equal hours, the day consisting of twenty-four hours of equal length throughout the year. Such hours have always been used in astronomical calculations, but in ordinary life, both in the East and in the West, people reckoned by temporal hours, i.e. day hours which were long in summer and short in winter. The increasing use of mechanical clocks and watches lead to the same results in the Christian and the Muhammadan world: the temporal hours died out in ordinary life and the equal hours took their place [3]. In Turkey the situation was somewhat different; equal hours were commonly used, but one counted twice twelve hours from sunset to sunset, which meant that clocks had to be set practically

---

[1] E. Wiedemann & J. Frank, 'Die Gebetszeiten im Islam', *Sitzungsberichte d. phys.-med. Sozietät zu Erlangen*, 58/59, 1928, 1-32. R. R. J. Rohr, 'Sonnenuhr und Astrolabium im Dienst der Moschee', *Centaurus*, 18, 1973, 44-56.

[2] J. Würschmidt, 'Die Schriften Gedosis über die Höhenparallelen und die Sinustafel (Zum Gebrauch des Quadranten im Islam)', *Sitzungsberichte d. phys.-med. Sozietät zu Erlangen*, 60, 1928, 127-154.

[3] G. Bilfinger, *Die mittelalterlichen Horen und die modernen Stunden*, 1892, 157 ff. C. M. Cipolla, *Clocks and Culture, 1300-1700*, 1967, 103 f.

every day [1]. These were the hours *alla turca* as distinct from the Western (*alla franca*) [2].

Clocks had become an essential element in the Westernization of the East. In the treaty concluded in 1808 between France and Persia Napoleon undertook to send the Shah craftsmen in many branches, among them *horlogers capable de faire des pendules* [3].

5. Musical Clocks

Musical clocks were, after watches and pendulums, the third profitable line in the export trade of the English clockmakers. Henton Brown, one of whose Turkish clocks is shown in Fig. 27, became a freeman of the Clockmakers' Company in 1726, master in 1753, and died in 1775. The clock with its Ionic columns follows a traditional pattern, but is decorated in a way to appeal to a Turkish buyer [4]. Crescents crown the finials in the four corners and on the cupola, while the decoration in lacquer painting (*japanning* is the old term) carefully avoids all figural subjects. The naturalistic flowers, although painted in England, would have appeared quite familiar to a Turk, as a similar style of naturalistic floral ornament was then in vogue there. And when the owner wished to listen to the chimes, he had the choice of six different tunes: two with Turkish titles [5], and two which are simply called "Air Turque", while the first and the last tune on the dial address themselves to the Christian minority in the Turkish Empire, being a *Romeaca*, a folk dance which seems to have found few admirers outside Greece [6], and an "Air Greek".

[1]   Bilfinger, *l.c.*, 196-199 ('Die türkische Uhr') suspects Western influence.

[2]   Modern Swiss firms produce wrist watches with two dials, one with Islamic, the other with Western numbers. It is said that they are intended for "Muslims a long way from Mecca so that they can follow religious rites by the time there" (E. Bruton, *Clocks and Watches*, 1968, 119). Pocket watches of this type have been manufactured for a hundred years or more; my guess is that they were intended to show the hours *alla turca* and *alla franca*.

[3]   *The Consolidated Treaty Series*, ed. C. Parry, vol. 54, 1969, 456.

[4]   P. G. Dawson, 'Clocks Made for the Turkish Market', *The Antique Collector*, 16, 1945, 211. Sale Sotheby's, April 27, 1970, lot 117. Dawson has reproduced two other Turkish clocks by Henton Brown, one of which had "since its re-importation" its Islamic chapter-ring replaced by one with Western numerals.

[5]   One is called "Uschac Deuir", i.e. uşşak, the name of a mode in Turkish music.

[6]   "La Musica coltivata da' Greci in Costantinopoli a' nostri dì, eccetto l'Eccle-

The elegant musical clock (Fig. 28a, b) of red tortoiseshell with ormolu mounts in rocaille style brought Western art forms and Western music to Turkey [1]. It is signed "Recordon Spencer & Perkins London". Louis Recordon, who was of Swiss origin, but worked all his life in London, also produced a number of watches for the Turkish market [2]. His association with the firm of Spencer & Perkins lasted from 1775 to 1794 [3]. The selection dial leaves one with the choice between Gigue, Dance, Minuetto, or Song. This might seem a surprising repertory for a Turkish home, but it is a fact that export clocks with Eastern tunes are the exception; the majority chime European favourites, usually including that embodiment of eighteenth-century grace, the minuet. Just at the time when in Europe the *rondo alla turca* sounded, when military music was modelled on that of the Janissaries, and the rhythm of the kettledrums was admitted even into church music, people on the Bosphorus listened in their homes to Western tunes.

This otherwise completely Western clock shows Islamic numbers and an enamel roundel with a picture of the Kaʿba, the holiest place in Islam, in the direction of which a Muhammadan must say his prayers at certain hours of the day (see p. 69). Schematized pictures of the Kaʿba were very popular in Turkey [4]. In the eighteenth century a European artist got hold of one of these views and redrew it according to the rules of perspective. The inclusion of his improved version in Bernard Picart's widely

siastica, che mostra dell'arte, e la *Romeca* che poco vale, è musica tutto Turchesca" (G. Toderini, *Letteratura turchesca*, 1781, I, 230). And Byron speaks of "the stupid Romaika, the dull round-about of the Greeks" (*Childe Harold's Pilgrimage*, canto II, Note on Albania).

[1] Here reproduced from two photographs which I owe to the kindness of Dr. Yvonne Hackenbroch who published the clock in her book *English Furniture in the Irwin Untermyer Collection*, 1958, 11. Dawson, *l.c.*, 208 f. Sale Christie's, December 12, 1972, 90.

[2] They are signed sometimes alone, sometimes combined with the names "Markwick Markham".

[3] These dates after Hackenbroch, *l.c.*

[4] R. Ettinghausen, 'Die bildliche Darstellung der Kaʿba im Islamischen Kulturkreis', *Zeitschrift der Deutschen Morgenländischen Gesellschaft*, 87, 1934, 111-137. K.Erdmann, 'Kaʿbah-Fliesen', *Ars Orientalis*, 3, 1959, 192-197.

read *Cérémonies et coûtumes religieuses* (1737) secured for it a wide circulation (Fig. 29) [1]. Picart's engraving was copied, not only on our clock but also, somewhat unexpectedly, in Japan (Fig. 30). The Japanese panel, painted in gold on black lacquer, belongs to a long and now widely scattered series of views of famous buildings and portraits of famous men, which a Dutchman, Baron van Reede, commissioned from native artists when he stayed in Japan in the years 1788-1789 [2].

Brown and Recordon were not the only English firms which shipped musical clocks to Turkey. Many other names appear on the dials: Benjamin Barber, Robert Best, Henry Borrell, George Clarke, Robert Markham, Richard Peckover, Markwick-Markham-Perigal, Francis Perigal, George Prior, Isaac Rogers, Daniel Torin, Vulliamy. But what do these names mean? Clocks are the product of team-work, and musical clocks naturally even more so as specialists have to be called in for the music mechanism. Here, however, more than just some outside help is implied; it seems that most of these musical clocks came from a few specialist workshops.

In 1967 Eric Bruton wrote [3]: "There is considerable similarity among the movements of musical clocks of the late eighteenth century for the Turkish market and it seems reasonably certain that they were all made by the same supplier, Thwaites and Reed of Clerkenwell, despite different makers' names on the dials". This is amply confirmed by the Day-books of this still existing firm, which are now in the Guildhall Library (Ms. 6788). These Day-books start in 1780 and show that Thwaites and Reed did indeed supply "the trade" with musical clocks for the Turkish market; not just the movements or barrels, but the complete clocks in their decorated cases ready for dispatch. Most of the famous clockmakers of the time appear among their customers.

---

[1] Vol. 5, pl. f. p. 70; in the English edition of 1739 vol. 7, pl. f. p. 34. Here reproduced from an anonymous English engraving which I owe to the kindness of my colleague Dr. Elizabeth McGrath.

[2] M. Feddersen, *Japanese Decorative Art*, 1962, 198 ff.

[3] E. Bruton, *Clocks and Watches, 1400-1900*, 1967, 125.

The firm of Spencer & Perkins paid on August 2, 1782 for "Three Eight Day Clocks with White Diall Plates Engraved in Turky Characters & Engraved at the Corners wit large Pendlums Engraved & Varnishd". Mr. Recordon paid (February 10, 1788) for "Two Spring One Tune Clocks within Jappan'd Plates ... The two Cases ... Jappan'd for the Turky Trade & with Festoon Corners", and Mr. Isaac Rogers on March 14, 1789 for "A New Spring Six Tune Chime Clock ... Centre Enamell for the Hours with Turky Characters". George Prior, the towering figure in the Turkey trade, was one of their best customers. His name appears time and again in the ledgers. On September 14, 1790 he paid for "A Pair of Spring four Tune clocks with 6 in. Diall Plates & a double row of Shipping in the Arch, with the Chime Barill ... fitted into Tortishell Cases for the Turky Market", together with two "Six Tune Clocks" in satin-wood cases, in addition to some repair work. How well organised the trade was one can see from the fact that a musical clock sent back from Turkey for repairs was put in order and "fitted into a New Jappand Case to go back to Turky". On March 9, 1797 George Prior was charged "To a small organ with 2 stops of metal pipes & Double Bellowes to play a piece of Turkish Music in 5 parts with one Train of Wheels & Double Springs in the Barrell & Chain to the Fuzey & with a Train of Running Work up to the cupalo (sic) of the Case to carry Round a Ring of 6 Figures all of which move as they pass Round. Viz. A Lion to open His Mouth & move His Tail. A Tyger to open His Mouth. A Bear to move His Head. A Hyena to move His Tail. A Horse to move His Head. A Stag to move His Head. All done by Leavers inside the Body of each animal & all properly painted & properly packed". Two years later (July 26, 1799) George Prior received a similar musical clock which he had ordered, only this time a wolf and and a crocodile replaced the hyena and the horse.

The English dominated the Turkish market as far as clocks were concerned, but they did not hold a monopoly. The inexpensive wooden musical clocks from the Black Forest region were imported from the third quarter of the eighteenth century onwards [1]. According to a contemporary source they had specially made dials, played Turkish music, and were decorated with the customary crescents and—surprisingly—with figures in Turkish dress; one would have thought that the buyers of these cheap clocks were conservative-minded and would object to figural representations.

Eventually the makers of musical clocks had to move with the times and replace the old-fashioned carillon with a new mechanism, the comb with flexible steel blades. Breguet exported such clocks to Turkey. In 1818 Leroy, his agent in Istanbul, reported [2]: "Leur jeu a été très goûté, lors de notre visite chez Allet Effendi, cependant nous avons remarqué que les airs étaient beaucoup trop courts et les sons trop doux; l'ameublement des grands salons turcs est de nature à affaiblir les sons. Aussi les jeux de flûtes anciens sont-ils aigus; les artistes qui nous ont précédés paraissent en cela s'être conformé au goût du pays".

[1]   F. Steyrer, *Geschichte der Schwarzwälder Uhrmacherkunst*, 1796, 43-46.
[2]   A. Chapuis, *Histoire de la boîte à musique*, 1955, figs. 266-267, p. 276.

CHAPTER IV

THE NINETEENTH CENTURY

1. Swiss Automata Watches and Singing Birds

In the early years of the nineteenth century the English musical clock gave way to the Swiss watches with automata, and to the "Singing Bird" musical boxes in their various shapes. It was not a sudden change as animated landscapes or animals in motion had already featured on some of the musical clocks.

Only in our age of "functional" timekeepers has it become necessary to remind ourselves that all through the centuries since Hellenistic times, in the East and in the West, clocks had often been combined with music and with moving mechanical figures. It was a triumph of Swiss ingenuity that this could now be achieved within the diminutive space of a pocket watch. At the same time the most efficiently organised team-work of specialists in watchmaking, musical movements, and enamel painting made sure that every watch or box was a perfect work of art.

Occasionally one finds such Swiss automata watches with Islamic numerals, like a gold-watch-*cum*-musical-box with the figure of a rope-dancer. When the music sounds, the little acrobat goes through his act, and two musicians move their hands to create the illusion as if the sound were coming from their tiny instruments [1]. At first sight one might be tempted to think that the subject was specially chosen for Turkish clients. For a long time Turkish acrobats had been travelling in Europe as performers on the tight-rope [2], but when the watch was made this difficult

---

[1] Formerly in the M. Sandoz Collection. Signed: Perrin Frères (active at Neuchâtel in the early 19th century). A. Chapuis and E. Droz, *Automata*, 1958, figs. 197-199. *A Loan Exhibition of Antique Automatons*, New York, A la Vieille Russie, Inc., 1950, No. 129, figs. 30 and 46.

[2] M. And, *Kirk gün kirk gece*, 1959, 117. In the sixteenth century Paolo Giovio included in his portrait gallery of famous people "Hali Turco funambulo" (*Periodico della Società storica per la Provincia e antica Diocesi di Como*, 16, 1904, 56).

and dangerous act was no longer a Turkish speciality, and rope-dancers were evidently a favourite subject with Swiss watch-makers [1].

Ancient Greek engineers had invented the mechanical singing birds: compressed air passing through a pipe emitted a whistling sound. This idea, which in Roman times led to the invention of the organ, was taken up in every age. The eighteenth century was a revolutionary age even in this field. Now for the first time birds learned their songs from man-made automata. Canaries which were outstanding singers were highly prized, but it was a most tedious job to train them, to whistle the same tune from morning to night for many months. Just then somebody invented the *serinette*, a kind of small organ constructed expressly for that very purpose.

A very gifted maker of clocks and automata at La Chaux-de-Fonds, Pierre Jaquet-Droz (1721-1790), had the idea that the mechanism of the clockwork singing birds could be improved in many ways. He succeeded in imitating to perfection the song of various birds, and, to make the illusion complete, he made the little performers move their heads, wings and tails with amazing realism. His work was continued, and even improved upon, by his son Henry-Louis (1752-1791) and by Jean-Frédéric Leschot (1746-1824) who founded a firm at Geneva. In the third quarter of the eighteenth century the Jaquet-Droz supplied James Cox, a London dealer, with such singing birds. James Cox calculated rightly that extremely rich and very complicated clock-automata would prove irresistible to wealthy Easterners. Although some of these automata incorporate figures of Turks, they aim only at a general impression of Oriental style. Cox was successful in selling many of them in China, especially to the Emperor himself, but he was apparently little interested in the Near Eastern market [2].

Pierre Jaquet-Droz, on the other hand, exported his automata

---

[1]   Examples can be seen in A. Chapuis and E. Gélis, *Le monde des automates*, 1928, II, figs. 324-326.

[2]   On him see C. Le Corbeiller, 'James Cox: a Biographical Review', *The Burlington Magazine*, 112, 1970, 351-358.

both to China and to Turkey. A report on them in the *Almanach de Gotha* for 1789 says: "In his workshop I have seen artificial canaries hopping about in cages and singing different songs, moving their beaks, throats and bodies naturally. He sends them to Constantinople and has already sold a large number to the Seraglio of the Grand Turk" [1]. In the Saray are still some such cages with singing birds combined with clocks; whether any of them are by Jaquet-Droz is impossible to say [2].

The work of the two Jaquet-Droz and of Leschot was continued with equal mastery by the brothers Ami-Napoléon and Louis Rochat at Geneva, whose singing birds acquired international fame in the first quarter of the nineteenth century. Their ambition was always to achieve the seemingly impossible. The watch (Fig. 31) looks ordinary enough, but inside a singing bird is hidden. It comes out from a slide in the edge at VI, while a second slide at II opens to let in air for the bellows and let out the sound [3]. In spite of the Roman numerals on the dial the watch was specially made for Turkey as becomes evident from the "Bosphorus landscape" on the back.

To surprise the beholder the birds often appear in unexpected places. The gorgeous large (29.5 cm.) mirror of gold and enamel (Fig. 32) has a flower on top. When one presses the handle the petals of the flower open, out comes a little bird, sings his song and disappears again. The "Bosphorus landscape" at the back is intended to add to the appeal for a Turkish buyer. The mirror is dated 1818 and signed with the initials FR [4].

The Rochat Brothers also produced a small number of richly chased and decorated pistols with tiny watches in their butts.

[1]   Quoted by Chapuis and Droz, *l.c.*, 214, who quote also from the correspondence of Jaquet-Droz with Pinel, his agent at Istanbul.

[2]   Chapuis and Droz, *l.c.*, figs. 259, 261.

[3]   From the collection of Sir David Salomons who had acquired it from Desoutter in 1922. Signed with the initials FR (Frères Rochat) and numbered 202. Chapuis & Gélis, *Le monde des automates*, 1928, II, 122, fig. 400. E. Jaquet and A. Chapuis, *Technique and History of the Swiss Watch*, 1953, 173 f., pl. 104.

[4]   Chapuis and Gélis, *l.c.*, II, 125 ff., figs. 402-403 and colour plate. *A Loan Exhibition of Antique Automatons*, New York, A la Vieille Russie, Inc., 1950, No. 164. *Musée d'horlogerie de la Ville de Locle*, 1967, No. 26.

The pistols are very harmless; they serve as scent sprinklers or a humming bird emerges briefly and sings. One of these extraordinary pistols is exhibited at the Saray among the enamels, not among the clocks and watches, but it has a small watch with "Turkish" numerals in the butt. When one presses the trigger a flower shoots out of the barrel, and sprays perfume. These pistols would be the limit of absurdity had one not to admire the impeccable taste and the perfection of their workmanship [1].

In the fifties of the nineteenth century the *Compagnie neuchâteloise d'exportation* discovered a new market for musical boxes, Persia, where they still had all the attractions of a novelty [2].

2. BREGUET

In Thackeray's novel *Vanity Fair* Amelia remarks one day quite casually that her watch can no longer be trusted. Off goes Major Dobbin, hopelessly in love, to get for her the best watches money can buy, one by Le Roy, the other by Breguet. A Turk, provided he had the necessary money, would have experienced no difficulty in buying watches by these two illustrious makers, and even examples specially made for the Eastern market.

Abraham Louis Breguet (1747-1823), the "Stradivarius of watchmaking" (R. T. Gould), regarded his Turkish clientèle as important enough to employ a sales agent, a certain Leroy, in Istanbul. Every single one of his watches and clocks was an individual masterpiece, and his Turkish customers were willing to pay the high prices demanded for perfection. Breguet incorporated in his Turkish watches his many new inventions, such as the "parachute" or "elastic suspension" which prevented damage to the watch caused by sudden shocks, or the combination with a thermometric scale. Even unusual types such as a centre-seconds stop-watch found buyers in Turkey [3].

Breguet's Turkish watches are of his normal austere type and

---

[1]   On these pistols see especially A. Chapuis, *Montres et émaux de Genève*, 1944, 189.

[2]   On the success of Swiss musical boxes in Persia see A. Chapuis, *Histoire de la boîte à musique*, 1955, 278 ff.

[3]   Sotheby's, July 23, 1962, No. 59.

make no concessions to a supposed Oriental taste for opulence; but everything is of impeccable workmanship. Even the Arabic has been written by an expert hand [1]. As with his watches for the European market, cases with pictorial decoration are the exception, but he gave in to the demand for "Bosphorus landscapes" [2]. One guesses that he would have preferred to do without enamel paintings, but he approved of maps as a decoration of the watch-case. However, as the maps of Turkey on Breguet watches show Greece as an independent state, they must date from after 1830, when after the death of its founder (1823) the firm of Breguet was continued by his son and grandson [3].

We have already mentioned Breguet's musical clocks [4]. Here too his fertile mind produced new and surprising ideas. In his famous *sympathiques* Breguet had connected the mechanisms of a clock and a watch, i.e. at night one fixed to the clock one's pocket watch which was then automatically set to the correct time of the clock. Breguet's musical clock of 1816 was also based on a "sympathy" between clock and watch: when going to bed one fixed the watch to the clock which then acted as *grande et petite sonnerie*, sounding hours, half hours and quarters [5].

Several French watchmakers, when signing their works, proudly added to their names the words "pupil of Breguet". On numerous "Turkish" watches one can read "Le Roy, élève de Breguet". This brings us to the yet unsolved problem of Le Roy watches. The name Le Roy or Leroy occurs often in the annals of horology. Julien Le Roy (1686-1759) and his son Pierre (1717-1785) were two of the most famous watchmakers of the eighteenth century. In the nineteenth century firms of this name

---

[1]   This applies also to the perfection with which the tughra of Sultan Mahmud (1808-1839) appears on one of Breguet's watches (Christie's, July 16, 1974, No. 345, reprod.).

[2]   See below, p. 95. *Musée d'horlogerie de la Ville de Locle*, 1967, 63, No. 805 (dated 1820). A. Chapuis, *A.-L. Breguet pendant la Révolution Française*, 1953, reproduces as frontispiece a Turkish Breguet watch of 1817 (from the Wilsdorf Collection) with a landscape which looks more European than Eastern.

[3]   L. Pippa, *Masterpieces of Watchmaking*, 1969, 178 f.

[4]   Above, p. 88.

[5]   C. Breguet, *A. L. Breguet horloger*, 1963, 26 f.

flourished both in Paris and in London. It is therefore not surprising to find the name Le Roy on a considerable number of watches made for the Turkish market. The watches signed with this name, and we shall assume that everybody who used this name was entitled to do so, fall into a few groups.

For a long time the great Julien Le Roy was credited with a group of Turkish watches which can be easily recognized by the ample use of enamel on the dial, by a curious predilection for green, as well as by the raised bands of chapters for the hours and minutes. Only a short while ago it was pointed out that these watches must be the work of "another Julien Le Roy" [1]. Is this the same man as the "Jln. Le Roy à Paris" whose watches are decorated on the reverse with "Bosphorus landscapes" and which date from the first quarter of the nineteenth century [2]?

Then there is a Charles Le Roy who must have been active at about the same time [3], and who is probably identical with the founder of the firm of *Leroy et Cie*. There is also "Leroy Horer. du Roi, a Paris", who is too reticent to reveal his first name. He was active when the "Bosphorus landscapes" were in vogue, and, as his title shows, certainly after the restoration of the French monarchy [4]. Or is he identical with one of the preceding watchmakers?

Our "Leroy, élève de Breguet" is another elusive personality. One suspects that he is the Leroy who acted as Breguet's agent in Istanbul from ca.1811 to 1818. Some of his signed watches are signed a second time on the dial in Arabic script (Fig. 33). The fine enamel decoration of a vase and flowers on the back recurs on a number of similar watches. He also produced a number of very

---

[1]   G. Brusa and C. Allix, 'Julien and Pierre Le Roy. Their business, their relations and their namesakes', *Antiquarian Horology*, June 1972, 598 f., where one of the two watches in the British Museum is reproduced. The authors say: "We believe them to be the work of the Julien who—according to Baillie—was born in 1738. We doubt whether they are entirely French". Another of these watches belongs to the Pitt-Rivers Museum in Oxford (1940-7.55).
[2]   A typical example was in the sale at Christie's, July 5, 1971, 181, and again at Sotheby's, March 27, 1972, 129.
[3]   Sotheby's, October 16, 1961, No. 76.
[4]   An example in the sale at Christie's, March 10, 1964, 116.

small watches, signed only in Arabic, with enamelled backs which are divided into segments and filled with flowers, quivers, and scientific and musical instruments (Fig. 34a, b) [1].

3. The Romantic Spirit and New Fashions

We have already had occasion to mention the "Bosphorus landscapes" which became fashionable in the early years of the nineteenth century [2]. The discovery of the "Beauties of the Bosphorus" came in the wake of the search for the Picturesque which had started in eighteenth-century England. Travellers went round the world in search of "picturesque scenery" which had remained unobserved, and landscape painters found new sources of inspiration.

In the case of Istanbul it was not really a new discovery. The incomparable skyline of Istanbul and the beauty of its surroundings had long been enchanting Turks and their foreign visitors. But as the Turks had no landscape painters, somebody conceived the idea of providing them with views of their beauty spots, not canvasses to be hung on a wall, but small enamel paintings decorating, within a scalloped frame, the cases of gold watches. With a simple technical trick Claude-like effects of sunrise and sunset were achieved: the sky of translucent pink enamel let the gold ground shine through and thus gave the illusion of the sun hidden behind layers of mist, while the rays of the sun engraved in the gold helped to reinforce the effect.

Large numbers of English, French and Swiss watches are decorated with such "Bosphorus landscapes", all in the same style which suggests that they all came from the same centre. This was in all likelihood Geneva where the art of enamelling

---

[1] A "Turkish" watch in the Uhrenmuseum, Vienna (from the Ebner-Eschenbach Collection) is signed on the dial in Arabic letters "Leroy"; the segmented back is enamelled with the usual scientific and musical instruments, flowers and quivers, while the movement is the work of Blondel and Melly at Geneva. The watch has been reproduced in colour in two books by H. Lunardi, *Rundgang durch das Uhrenmuseum der Stadt Wien*, 1973, pl. 4, and *Alte Wiener Uhren und ihr Museum*, 1973, pl. 4. Normally Blondel and Melly seem to have exported watches under their own name.
[2] See above, pp. 91 and 93 f.

watch cases had flourished continually since its beginning in the seventeenth century. The fashion for the "Bosphorus landscapes" started around 1810 and lasted several decades. As well as on watches, such enamel landscapes also occur on snuffboxes, the Turks having learned from the French the habits of taking snuff, of carrying it in costly decorated little boxes, and of the monarch's distributing such boxes as tokens of honour and distinction [1]. The snuffboxes show not only the same types of landscape, but often the same décor of flowers, trophies, scientific and musical instruments as the watches, and were evidently produced by the same painters.

Sometimes one finds on these watches identifiable views of Istanbul such as the Saray or the Hagia Sophia, but much more often the scene depicted is the coastline of the Bosphorus with sailing ships, mosques and minarets. Some of these views are evidently based on sketches made on the spot, but in the vast majority the aim was simply to evoke the general impression of a Mediterranean shore. Even this can change into a Central European lake scene, often of a distinctly Swiss character. It seems that the real "Bosphorus landscapes" were used exclusively on watches for the Turkish market; this would apply even to the rare instances where the dial shows European chapters (see above, p. 91).

Much more surprising is the vogue for Neo-Gothic clocks in nineteenth-century Turkey, especially as their religious and nationalistic undertones, neo-Catholicism and the evocation of the Middle Ages, were completely meaningless there (Fig. 35) [2]. Westernization simply meant taking up the latest Parisian fashion.

There was nothing retrospective in the fashion for skeleton clocks which began in France and spread to Turkey in the nineteenth century [3]. Quite on the contrary, it was the most revolu-

---

[1]   H. and S. Berry-Hill, *Antique Gold Boxes. Their Lore and Their Lure*, 1960, 159.

[2]   In the Museum at Zagreb. *Chamber Clocks. Exhibition of Clocks from Yugoslav Collections*, Beograd, Museum of Applied Arts, 1964, No. 98.

[3]   F. B. Royer-Collard, *Skeleton Clocks*, 1969, deals with English and French examples. Turkish skeleton clocks are reproduced by P. Ülkümen, Saatçiliğimiz, *Türk Etnografya Dergisi*, 4, 1961, 14 ff.

tionary step in design to dispense entirely with the artistically decorated case of the clock which hid the movement, and to make the rotating wheels and pinions the centre of attraction.

In a Muhammadan country it was an even more revolutionary step to have watches with the portrait of the reigning sultan. This happened first under Sultan Abdülmecid (1839-1861). The watch (Fig. 36a-e) is the product of the firm of Auguste Courvoisier & Cie. at La Chaux-de-Fonds [1]; the portrait of the Sultan is in the best tradition of Swiss enamel painting, and must date from the fifties of the nineteenth century [2]. A watch with an identical portrait belongs to the palace collection in the Saray. The fashion for watches with the portrait of the Sultan lasted almost until the end of the monarchy, but under Mehmed V (1909-1918), the last but one of the Turkish Sultans, the art of miniature painting was already dead and a photographic likeness took its place.

4. Edward Prior

While the more sophisticated Turks preferred the latest Parisian fashion in clocks and watches, there existed in Turkey as elsewhere a large body of conservative people, who asked for good solid watches of the type grandfather used to wear. Edward Prior, George's son, catered just for these customers. Father and son together provided the Turks with over seventy-eight thousand watches.

Here time stood still, if one may use this phrase in connection with watches. The watch shown in Fig. 37 is by its serial number (73,753) and hallmark dated 1861. When it turned up in a sale a few years ago, the experienced cataloguer misread the hallmark as 1781, an error of exactly 80 years. It is a pardonable error because Prior watches always remained the same, solid but rather

---

[1]   Serial number 51,007. Galerie am Neumarkt, Zürich, *Uhren-Auktion*, October 3, 1969, No. 361.

[2]   It can be dated approximately by a medal of 1853 which shows the Sultan at about the same age, and with the same fez and aigrette (N. Pere, *Osmanlılarda Madenî Paralar*, 1968, No.1103).

monotonous. It is not quite true to say that they never changed, because in his last years Edward Prior occasionally replaced the verge with a cylinder escapement. Whether this was an advantage is doubtful; the old movement was probably easier to repair when the necessity arose.

During the last years of his activity Edward Prior put little slips of paper into his watch-cases which showed his own name and that of his father in Roman capitals, just as they appeared on the dials, and below them in Arabic characters the Turkish word for "son". Anyone who had doubts could rest assured that Edward Prior was the legitimate heir of his father's business.

Edward Prior continued the numbering of watches begun by his father. As collectors might want to date their watches at least approximately, I give here a few serial numbers of watches which are dated by their hallmarks:

    35,821 . . . . 1810 (Christie's, 20 February 1962, lot 60)
    50,554 . . . . 1833 (Christie's, 29 March 1960, lot 37)
    64,293 . . . . 1849 (British Museum, CAI-544)
    74,078 . . . . 1862 (Sotheby's, 8 December 1969, lot 77)
    78,012 . . . . 1869 (Sotheby's, 23 June 1969, lot 89)

For some years there was some overlapping. Sometimes a watch shows the name of the father, sometimes of the son. Rarely do we find one name on the dial, and the other on the movement[1]. Only in his youth, and even then only exceptionally, did he follow the practice of his father and buy signed movements from other watchmakers[2].

The last watches Edward Prior sent to Turkey date from 1869. Only twelve years later traffic started in the opposite direction. In 1891 we hear of one of the musical clocks which Isaac Rogers had made for the Turkish market being brought back to England[3].

---

[1]   British Museum (CAI-546), serial number 42,003; hallmark 1816; the movement signed by Edward Prior.

[2]   Watch hallmarked 1815, the movement by George Charle, the dial signed Edward Prior: Sotheby's, December 8, 1969, No. 79.

[3]   F. J. Britten, *Old Clocks and Watches and Their Makers*, 6th ed., 1932, 826.

Since then thousands of these clocks and watches have followed it. What the Turks discarded as old-fashioned and no longer needed found a ready market among English collectors as coming from a great period of English horology.

5. THE FIRST PUBLIC CLOCK

By the middle of the nineteenth century Istanbul possessed the first public clock built in an Islamic country, not a minaret but a secular building in that enchanting style where a native tradition blends harmoniously with the then fashionable French neo-Baroque (Fig. 38). The clock-tower (*saat kulesi*), wonderfully situated on the shores of the Bosphorus, belongs to a group of buildings which are connected with the Dolmabahçe Palace. Three hundred years earlier Busbecq had remarked on the absence of public clocks in Turkey, and why the religious party success-fully prevented their erection [1].

The statement that the Dolmabahçe clock-tower was the first of its kind needs qualification. Historians should always be conscious how risky it is to use the word "first". Clepsydras, especially those combined with mechanical figures, existed in public places both in classical antiquity and in the Islamic Middle Ages. But mechanical clocks on monumental buildings remained restricted to the Western world. The public clock on the market in Isfahan remained an isolated experiment, and not even a successful one [2]. After the death of the man who had constructed it, there was nobody who could keep it in working order.

There existed, however, a small number of clock-towers in Eastern Europe and the Balkans, parts of the Turkish empire with a preponderantly Christian population. Most of them were originally church-towers, relics from before the time of the Turkish conquest. This happened in Ofen (Budapest), where the clock was still striking the hours at the time of Evliya Çelebi's travels [3]. In the late sixteenth century Salomon Schweigger

[1] See above, p. 28.
[2] See above, p. 62.
[3] W. Björkman, *Ofen zur Türkenzeit*, 1920, 29 f.

observed: "They have neither bells nor clocks except at Gran and Ofen, where there are striking clocks, otherwise you don't find any in the whole of Turkey" [1]. This was not quite correct. The clock-tower at Üsküb (Skopje) is still in existence. A Turkish writer who visited Üsküb in 1593 mentions it among the "buildings of the infidels", albeit as one of the main sights of the town [2]. Still, such clocks were rare enough to attract the attention of travellers. When in 1587 Lubenau saw at Jagodina (in present-day Yugoslavia) a wooden tower with a striking clock, he was told that it was the work of a former ruling Bey who was originally a German clockmaker; he had made the clock with his own hands, had left money for its upkeep and instructed people how to service it [3].

While all these were relics of the Christian past of the Balkans, the clock-tower at Yenice Vardar (Giannitsa, now in Greece) proclaims itself proudly in its inscription as a pious Muhammadan foundation. It was erected in A.H. 1167 (A.D. 1753/54) and is still standing, unfortunately without the upper part which contained the clocks [4]. In Bosnia mosques with clock-towers were apparently not uncommon [5].

Not a forerunner, but a contemporary of the Istanbul clock-tower is the one in the Citadel of Cairo which was built in 1854 to house a clock which King Louis-Philippe of France had given to Muhammad Ali [6].

---

[1] S. Schweigger, *Ein newe Reyssbeschreibung*, 1608 (reprint 1964), 24.

[2] This was pointed out to me by my friend Paul Wittek. H. W. Duda, 'Balkantürkische Studien', *Sitzungsberichte der Österr. Akademie d. Wiss.*, 226, 1951, pp. 18, 28, 60 f., pl. 8, where Duda refers to other such towers. R. Anhegger, 'Neues zur balkantürkischen Forschung', *Zeitschrift der Deutschen Morgenländischen Gesellschaft*, 103, 1953, 82.

[3] R. Lubenau, *Beschreibung der Reisen*, I, 1914, 98.

[4] M. Kiel, 'Yenice Vardar', *Byzantina neerlandica*, fasc. 3, 1972, 321 ff., who mentions four other such clock-towers in Greece.

[5] A. Hangi, *Die Moslims in Bosnien-Hercegovina*, 1907, 17: "In grösseren Orten befindet sich neben den Hauptmoscheen auch ein Uhrturm (Sahat kula), dessen Uhr die Zeit à la Turcha angibt". *Alla turca* means twice twelve equal hours from sunset to sunset.

[6] G. Wiet, *Mohammed Ali et les beaux-arts*, n.d., 279 f., 285 f.

6. FINALE

Up to the end of the thirteenth century the superiority of Islamic technology remained unchallenged. It was technology based, and perhaps more than based, on the achievements of Greek engineers (which were forgotten in the West), but to which much had been added. How to find the hour of the day or the night by anything but the crudest means was a secret of the Islamic world. But in Christian Spain men already learned in the eleventh century from their Muhammadan neighbours what an astrolabe was and the many uses to which it could be put.

The thirteenth century in the West was an age of new ideas and experimentation as far as clock-making was concerned. When in the years around 1300 the first mechanical clocks appeared in the West, Islamic technology was already too fossilized to take note of this epoch-making invention. Only in the fifteenth century do we find a man open-minded enough to realize that his country had been left behind, and willing to make up for the time lost: this was the conqueror of Constantinople, Mehmet II. It remained an isolated attempt. The situation might have changed under Süleyman in the sixteenth century. But just then there was no need to invite foreign clockmakers to train native craftsmen. The Sultan's interest in clocks was genuine, and it was an extraordinary decision to insist that part of the foreign tribute must be paid in clocks; but it was just this tribute and the diplomatic gifts which provided the Saray with more masterpieces of Western horology than one could ever think of using.

Then, at last, in the seventeenth century the watchmakers of Galata, first foreigners, then Turks, produced watches as good as any produced in Europe in the early decades of the century. This was precisely their drawback. It seemed hopeless to keep pace with technological progress in the Western world. Horology did not stand still. On the contrary, in the second half of the century two inventions were made, the pendulum in clocks and the spring-balance in watches, which at last made exact time-keeping possible.

There were many other reasons why the budding industry in Istanbul was doomed. The watchmakers there worked for the local market. How could they compete with European industry in the age of mercantilism, and a veritable export drive by which the Western countries tried constantly to establish new markets in all continents?

The various Western nations distinguished themselves in different fields. The Swiss discovered the advantages of the division of labour: each village specialised in one part of the watch mechanism and achieved the highest standards in precision work. The English became famous for reliable quality, and Paris had early become the *arbiter elegantiarum*, the dictator of fashions in Europe as well as in the Near East. What chance was there of competing?

There is no proper ending to our story except to state that by the nineteenth century clocks and watches were freely available in the East. It was only in outlying regions that they retained their old attraction as desirable rareties. When in the Sudan in the wake of the Mahdi Revolt Slatin Pasha was forced to live as a prisoner of the Khalifa (1883-95), he tried to improve his condition by writing to Vienna for a dozen ordinary watches as he knew that they would serve as "most appreciated gifts as the Emirs lived in constant worry about the prayer hours which have to be punctually observed" [1].

Even before Atatürk abolished the Arabic alphabet and introduced the Latin (1928), he had already decreed the use of the European numerals, together with international time and the international calendar (1925). There was no longer any need to produce clocks and watches with dials specially designed for the "Turkish market". Naturally the reform did not affect the rest of the Muslim world, but by then watches had become so common and familiar that people merely looked at the position of the hands without having to read the numbers.

[1]   R. Slatin Pasha, *Feuer und Schwert im Sudan*, 1896, 399, 412. The Khalifa himself was fond of clocks. There existed at Omdurman an Armenian watchmaker who did repair work (*ibid.*, 537 f.).

"European Clocks and Watches in the Near East" is a chapter in the history of Western technology and of Eastern mental attitudes. The relationship, or as some might prefer to say the conflict, between the Near East and the West has been intensively studied in recent years, although the many books and papers dedicated to the subject all seem to concentrate on political systems and ideologies, and to avoid any discussion of technology, which holds a key position. Western technology has recently come under much criticism, not all of it unfounded, but all this criticism seems to have originated in the West. The observer of the modern political scene will have no difficulty in finding in the East any number of movements with a vehement anti-Western ideology, but it would be hard to discover among them a single one the adherents of which would reject the achievements and the comforts of Western technology.

INDEX

PLATES

PLATE I

Fig. 2.

Fig. 1.

Elephant Clock. Ms. dated A.D. 1315.

PLATE II

PLATE III

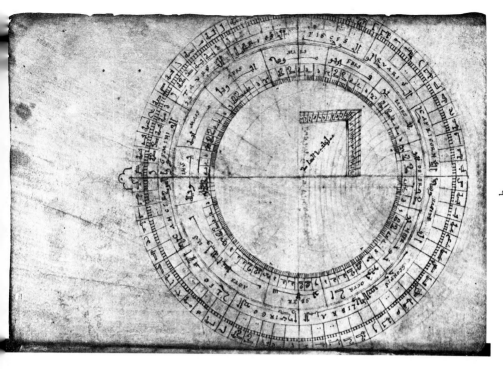

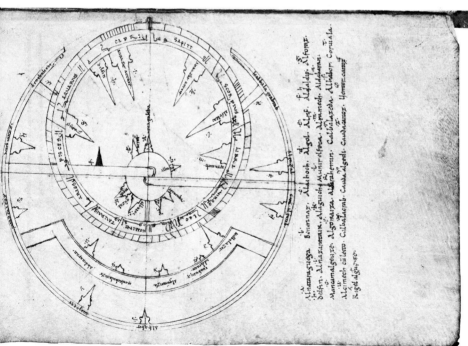

Fig. 4. Astrolabe (11th cent.) inscribed in Arabic and Latin.

PLATE IV

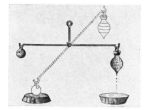

Fig. 5. Steelyard Water-
clock according to the
Zohar.

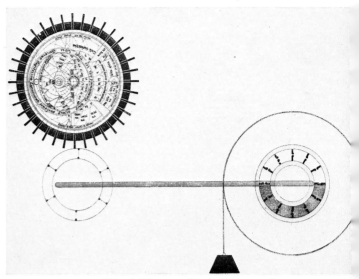

Fig. 6. Mercury Clock (13th cent.).

Fig. 7. Elephant Clock, ca. 1600.

PLATE V

Fig. 8. Presentation of a clock to the Sultan, 1574.

Fig. 9. Presentation of a clock to a Pasha, 1628.

PLATE VI

Fig. 10. Presentation of a clock to the Sultan, 1694.

Fig. 11. Clock with Turks (late 16th cent.).   Fig. 12. Clock with Sultan (late 16th cent.).

PLATE VII

Fig. 13a. Observatory of Taqī ad-Dīn.

Fig. 13b. Detail: clock.

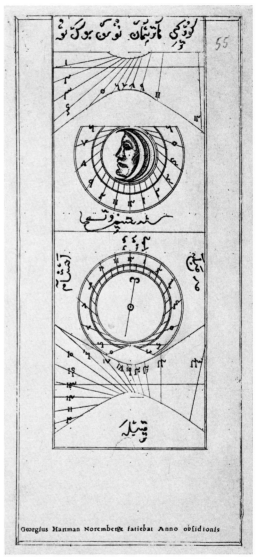

Fig. 14. Design for a sundial (1552).

Plate VIII

a   b

Fig. 15. Watch by Dūnā (17th cent.). London.

a   b

Fig. 16. Watch by Dūnā (17th cent.).
Kassel.

c   d

PLATE IX

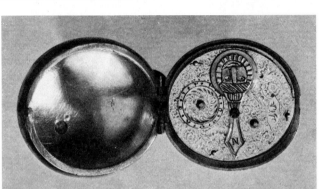

Fig. 18. Watch by Arlaud (17th cent.). Jerusalem.

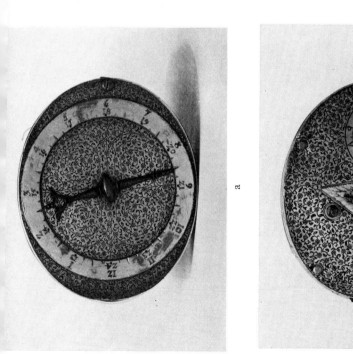

Fig. 17. Watch by Dūnā (17th cent.). Jerusalem.

PLATE X

Fig. 19. Clock by D. Buschmann (1626-1733). Augsburg.

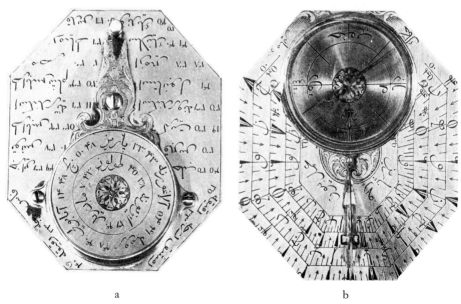

a   b

Fig. 20. Sundial by N. Brion (18th cent.). Greenwich.

PLATE XI

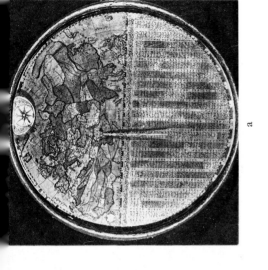

Fig. 22. *Qibla* indicator, 1738. Dublin.

a

b

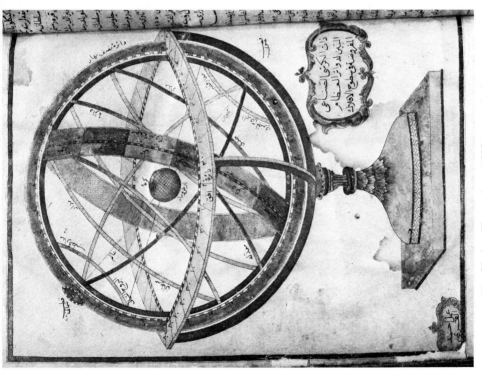

Fig. 21. Armillary sphere, 1732 (engraving).

PLATE XII

Fig. 23. Persians visiting a clockmaker (18th cent. painting). Besancon.

Fig. 24 Watch by Isaac Rogers, 1974. Jerusalem.

Fig. 25. Watch by Isaac Rogers. New York.

PLATE XIII

a   b   c

Fig. 26. Forgery of a watch by George Prior.

Fig. 27. Musical clock by H. Brown. Jerusalem.

PLATE XIV

a b

Fig. 28. Musical clock (English, 18th cent.). Jerusalem.

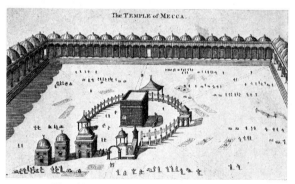

Fig. 29. Mecca (18th cent. engraving).

Fig. 30. Mecca (Japanese lacquer).

a   b   c   d

Fig. 31. Watch by the Brothers Rochat (early 19th cent.)

a   b

Fig. 33. Watch by Leroy. Jerusalem.

Fig. 32. Mirror by
Rochat.

a   b

Fig. 34. Watch by Leroy. Jerusalem

Fig. 35. Turkish Neo-Gothic
clock. Zagreb.

a   b   c

Fig. 36. Swiss watch, ca. 1853. Jerusalem.

Fig. 37. Watch by Edward Prior, 1861.
Jerusalem.

Fig. 38. Clock-tower, Istanbul.